Security Apps
Complete Self-Assessment Guide

The guidance in this Self-Assessment is based on Security Apps best practices and standards in business process architecture, design and quality management. The guidance is also based on the professional judgment of the individual collaborators listed in the Acknowledgments.

Notice of rights

Trademarks

Table of Contents

About The Art of Service

The Art of Service, Business Process Architects since 2000, is dedicated to helping stakeholders achieve excellence.

Defining, designing, creating, and implementing a process to solve a stakeholders challenge or meet an objective is the most valuable role... In EVERY group, company, organization and department.

Unless you're talking a one-time, single-use project, there should be a process. Whether that process is managed and implemented by humans, AI, or a combination of the two, it needs to be designed by someone with a complex enough perspective to ask the right questions.

Someone capable of asking the right questions and step back and say, 'What are we really trying to accomplish here? And is there a different way to look at it?'

With The Art of Service's Standard Requirements Self-Assessments, we empower people who can do just that — whether their title is marketer, entrepreneur, manager, salesperson, consultant, Business Process Manager, executive assistant, IT Manager, CIO etc... —they are the people who rule the future. They are people who watch the process as it happens, and ask the right questions to make the process work better.

Contact us when you need any support with this Self-Assessment and any help with templates, blue-prints and examples of standard documents you might need:

http://theartofservice.com
service@theartofservice.com

Acknowledgments

This checklist was developed under the auspices of The Art of Service, chaired by Gerardus Blokdyk.

Representatives from several client companies participated in the preparation of this Self-Assessment.

In addition, we are thankful for the design and printing services provided.

Included Resources - how to access

Included with your purchase of the book is the Security Apps Self-Assessment Spreadsheet Dashboard which contains all questions and Self-Assessment areas and auto-generates insights, graphs, and project RACI planning - all with examples to get you started right away.

How? Simply send an email to
access@theartofservice.com
with this books' title in the subject to get the Security Apps Self Assessment Tool right away.

You will receive the following contents with New and Updated specific criteria:

• The latest quick edition of the book in PDF

• The latest complete edition of the book in PDF, which criteria correspond to the criteria in...

• The Self-Assessment Excel Dashboard, and...

• Example pre-filled Self-Assessment Excel Dashboard to get familiar with results generation

• In-depth specific Checklists covering the topic

• Project management checklists and templates to assist with implementation

INCLUDES LIFETIME SELF ASSESSMENT UPDATES

Every self assessment comes with Lifetime Updates and Lifetime Free Updated Books. Lifetime Updates is an industry-first feature which allows you to receive verified self assessment updates, ensuring you always have the most accurate information at your fingertips.

Get it now- you will be glad you did - do it now, before you forget.

Send an email to **access@theartofservice.com** with this books' title in the subject to get the Security Apps Self Assessment Tool right away.

Your feedback is invaluable to us

If you recently bought this book, we would love to hear from you! You can do this by writing a review on amazon (or the online store where you purchased this book) about your last purchase! As part of our continual service improvement process, we love to hear real client experiences and feedback.

How does it work?
To post a review on Amazon, just log in to your account and click on the Create Your Own Review button (under Customer Reviews) of the relevant product page. You can find examples of product reviews in Amazon. If you purchased from another online store, simply follow their procedures.

What happens when I submit my review?
Once you have submitted your review, send us an email at review@theartofservice.com with the link to your review so we can properly thank you for your feedback.

Purpose of this Self-Assessment

This Self-Assessment has been developed to improve understanding of the requirements and elements of Security Apps, based on best practices and standards in business process architecture, design and quality management.

It is designed to allow for a rapid Self-Assessment to determine how closely existing management practices and procedures correspond to the elements of the Self-Assessment.

The criteria of requirements and elements of Security Apps have been rephrased in the format of a Self-Assessment questionnaire, with a seven-criterion scoring system, as explained in this document.

In this format, even with limited background knowledge of

Security Apps, a manager can quickly review existing operations to determine how they measure up to the standards. This in turn can serve as the starting point of a 'gap analysis' to identify management tools or system elements that might usefully be implemented in the organization to help improve overall performance.

How to use the Self-Assessment

On the following pages are a series of questions to identify to what extent your Security Apps initiative is complete in comparison to the requirements set in standards.

To facilitate answering the questions, there is a space in front of each question to enter a score on a scale of '1' to '5'.

1 Strongly Disagree

2 Disagree

3 Neutral

4 Agree

5 Strongly Agree

Read the question and rate it with the following in front of mind:

'In my belief, the answer to this question is clearly defined'.

There are two ways in which you can choose to interpret this statement;
1. how aware are you that the answer to the question is clearly defined
2. for more in-depth analysis you can choose to gather

evidence and confirm the answer to the question. This obviously will take more time, most Self-Assessment users opt for the first way to interpret the question and dig deeper later on based on the outcome of the overall Self-Assessment.

A score of '1' would mean that the answer is not clear at all, where a '5' would mean the answer is crystal clear and defined. Leave emtpy when the question is not applicable or you don't want to answer it, you can skip it without affecting your score. Write your score in the space provided.

After you have responded to all the appropriate statements in each section, compute your average score for that section, using the formula provided, and round to the nearest tenth. Then transfer to the corresponding spoke in the Security Apps Scorecard on the second next page of the Self-Assessment.

Your completed Security Apps Scorecard will give you a clear presentation of which Security Apps areas need attention.

Security Apps
Scorecard Example

Example of how the finalized Scorecard can look like:

Security Apps
Scorecard

Your Scores:

BEGINNING OF THE SELF-ASSESSMENT:

CRITERION #1: RECOGNIZE

INTENT: Be aware of the need for change. Recognize that there is an unfavorable variation, problem or symptom.

In my belief, the answer to this question is clearly defined:

5 Strongly Agree

4 Agree

3 Neutral

2 Disagree

1 Strongly Disagree

1. When a Security Apps manager recognizes a problem, what options are available?
<--- Score

2. Looking at each person individually – does every one have the qualities which are needed to work in this group?
<--- Score

3. How do you recognize an Security Apps objection?
<--- Score

4. What training and capacity building actions are needed to implement proposed reforms?
<--- Score

5. Whom do you really need or want to serve?
<--- Score

6. Who should resolve the Security Apps issues?
<--- Score

7. For your Security Apps project, identify and describe the business environment, is there more than one layer to the business environment?
<--- Score

8. Is it clear when you think of the day ahead of you what activities and tasks you need to complete?
<--- Score

9. What needs to be done?
<--- Score

10. What prevents you from making the changes you know will make you a more effective Security Apps leader?
<--- Score

11. What situation(s) led to this Security Apps Self Assessment?
<--- Score

12. Are controls defined to recognize and contain problems?

<--- Score

13. What should be considered when identifying available resources, constraints, and deadlines?
<--- Score

14. How are you going to measure success?
<--- Score

15. What are the timeframes required to resolve each of the issues/problems?
<--- Score

16. How many trainings, in total, are needed?
<--- Score

17. What are your needs in relation to Security Apps skills, labor, equipment, and markets?
<--- Score

18. Are there regulatory / compliance issues?
<--- Score

19. What is the extent or complexity of the Security Apps problem?
<--- Score

20. Do you need different information or graphics?
<--- Score

21. What problems are you facing and how do you consider Security Apps will circumvent those obstacles?
<--- Score

22. Will new equipment/products be required to

facilitate Security Apps delivery, for example is new software needed?

<--- Score

23. Is it needed?

<--- Score

24. Would you recognize a threat from the inside?

<--- Score

25. Have you identified your Security Apps key performance indicators?

<--- Score

26. What extra resources will you need?

<--- Score

27. What is the smallest subset of the problem you can usefully solve?

<--- Score

28. What Security Apps coordination do you need?

<--- Score

29. What are the clients issues and concerns?

<--- Score

30. What are the expected benefits of Security Apps to the stakeholder?

<--- Score

31. What needs to stay?

<--- Score

32. Is the quality assurance team identified?

<--- Score

33. Are problem definition and motivation clearly presented?
<--- Score

34. Why the need?
<--- Score

35. Are losses recognized in a timely manner?
<--- Score

36. What resources or support might you need?
<--- Score

37. Think about the people you identified for your Security Apps project and the project responsibilities you would assign to them, what kind of training do you think they would need to perform these responsibilities effectively?
<--- Score

38. Who defines the rules in relation to any given issue?
<--- Score

39. Do you recognize Security Apps achievements?
<--- Score

40. Are employees recognized for desired behaviors?
<--- Score

41. How does it fit into your organizational needs and tasks?
<--- Score

42. Are there any revenue recognition issues?

<--- Score

43. What is the Security Apps problem definition? What do you need to resolve?
<--- Score

44. What do you need to start doing?
<--- Score

45. Will a response program recognize when a crisis occurs and provide some level of response?
<--- Score

46. Where do you need to exercise leadership?
<--- Score

47. How are the Security Apps's objectives aligned to the group's overall stakeholder strategy?
<--- Score

48. Why is this needed?
<--- Score

49. How are training requirements identified?
<--- Score

50. Does Security Apps create potential expectations in other areas that need to be recognized and considered?
<--- Score

51. Will Security Apps deliverables need to be tested and, if so, by whom?
<--- Score

52. Can management personnel recognize the

monetary benefit of Security Apps?
<--- Score

53. Who else hopes to benefit from it?
<--- Score

54. Are your goals realistic? Do you need to redefine your problem? Perhaps the problem has changed or maybe you have reached your goal and need to set a new one?
<--- Score

55. Are employees recognized or rewarded for performance that demonstrates the highest levels of integrity?
<--- Score

56. Do you know what you need to know about Security Apps?
<--- Score

57. To what extent would your organization benefit from being recognized as a award recipient?
<--- Score

58. How do you identify the kinds of information that you will need?
<--- Score

59. Will it solve real problems?
<--- Score

60. What Security Apps problem should be solved?
<--- Score

61. Did you miss any major Security Apps issues?
<--- Score

62. Which needs are not included or involved?
<--- Score

63. What would happen if Security Apps weren't done?
<--- Score

64. How do you identify subcontractor relationships?
<--- Score

65. Are there Security Apps problems defined?
<--- Score

66. Who needs budgets?
<--- Score

67. How do you take a forward-looking perspective in identifying Security Apps research related to market response and models?
<--- Score

68. What information do users need?
<--- Score

69. What do employees need in the short term?
<--- Score

70. Is the need for organizational change recognized?
<--- Score

71. Do you have/need 24-hour access to key personnel?

<--- Score

72. Are there recognized Security Apps problems?
<--- Score

73. What creative shifts do you need to take?
<--- Score

74. What is the recognized need?
<--- Score

75. Who needs to know about Security Apps?
<--- Score

76. What is the problem or issue?
<--- Score

77. How do you assess your Security Apps workforce capability and capacity needs, including skills, competencies, and staffing levels?
<--- Score

78. What does Security Apps success mean to the stakeholders?
<--- Score

79. Consider your own Security Apps project, what types of organizational problems do you think might be causing or affecting your problem, based on the work done so far?
<--- Score

80. How do you recognize an objection?
<--- Score

81. Which information does the Security Apps

business case need to include?
<--- Score

82. Which issues are too important to ignore?
<--- Score

83. Where is training needed?
<--- Score

84. What Security Apps events should you attend?
<--- Score

85. What are the minority interests and what amount of minority interests can be recognized?
<--- Score

86. Do you need to avoid or amend any Security Apps activities?
<--- Score

87. What are the Security Apps resources needed?
<--- Score

88. How can auditing be a preventative security measure?
<--- Score

89. Are there any specific expectations or concerns about the Security Apps team, Security Apps itself?
<--- Score

90. As a sponsor, customer or management, how important is it to meet goals, objectives?
<--- Score

91. How much are sponsors, customers, partners,

stakeholders involved in Security Apps? In other words, what are the risks, if Security Apps does not deliver successfully?

<--- Score

92. What vendors make products that address the Security Apps needs?

<--- Score

93. Does the problem have ethical dimensions?

<--- Score

94. What Security Apps capabilities do you need?

<--- Score

95. What is the problem and/or vulnerability?

<--- Score

96. What are the stakeholder objectives to be achieved with Security Apps?

<--- Score

97. What activities does the governance board need to consider?

<--- Score

Add up total points for this section:
_ _ _ _ _ = Total points for this section

Divided by: _ _ _ _ _ _ (number of statements answered) = _ _ _ _ _ _
Average score for this section

Transfer your score to the Security Apps Index at the beginning of the Self-Assessment.

CRITERION #2: DEFINE:

In my belief, the answer to this question is clearly defined:

5 Strongly Agree

4 Agree

3 Neutral

2 Disagree

1 Strongly Disagree

1. How do you catch Security Apps definition inconsistencies?
<--- Score

2. Is there a completed, verified, and validated high-level 'as is' (not 'should be' or 'could be') stakeholder process map?
<--- Score

3. What is the definition of success?
<--- Score

4. Do the problem and goal statements meet the SMART criteria (specific, measurable, attainable, relevant, and time-bound)?
<--- Score

5. Is there any additional Security Apps definition of success?
<--- Score

6. How will the Security Apps team and the group measure complete success of Security Apps?
<--- Score

7. What is the scope of the Security Apps work?
<--- Score

8. Who defines (or who defined) the rules and roles?
<--- Score

9. When is/was the Security Apps start date?
<--- Score

10. Does the team have regular meetings?
<--- Score

11. What scope to assess?
<--- Score

12. Are improvement team members fully trained on Security Apps?
<--- Score

13. Will a Security Apps production readiness review

be required?
<--- Score

14. How do you gather Security Apps requirements?
<--- Score

15. What is a worst-case scenario for losses?
<--- Score

16. What is the worst case scenario?
<--- Score

17. In what way can you redefine the criteria of choice clients have in your category in your favor?
<--- Score

18. Who approved the Security Apps scope?
<--- Score

19. What happens if Security Apps's scope changes?
<--- Score

20. How is the team tracking and documenting its work?
<--- Score

21. What information do you gather?
<--- Score

22. What is in the scope and what is not in scope?
<--- Score

23. Is there regularly 100% attendance at the team meetings? If not, have appointed substitutes attended to preserve cross-functionality and full

representation?
<--- Score

24. Scope of sensitive information?
<--- Score

25. Has your scope been defined?
<--- Score

26. Are resources adequate for the scope?
<--- Score

27. Is the improvement team aware of the different versions of a process: what they think it is vs. what it actually is vs. what it should be vs. what it could be?
<--- Score

28. How do you manage unclear Security Apps requirements?
<--- Score

29. The political context: who holds power?
<--- Score

30. Is the team adequately staffed with the desired cross-functionality? If not, what additional resources are available to the team?
<--- Score

31. When are meeting minutes sent out? Who is on the distribution list?
<--- Score

32. Do you have a Security Apps success story or case study ready to tell and share?
<--- Score

33. Are all requirements met?
<--- Score

34. Have specific policy objectives been defined?
<--- Score

35. How would you define Security Apps leadership?
<--- Score

36. Has the Security Apps work been fairly and/
or equitably divided and delegated among team
members who are qualified and capable to perform
the work? Has everyone contributed?
<--- Score

37. What are the tasks and definitions?
<--- Score

38. How and when will the baselines be defined?
<--- Score

39. Are different versions of process maps needed to
account for the different types of inputs?
<--- Score

40. Will team members regularly document their
Security Apps work?
<--- Score

41. Is the Security Apps scope manageable?
<--- Score

42. Are the Security Apps requirements testable?
<--- Score

43. How do you manage scope?
<--- Score

44. What are the core elements of the Security Apps business case?
<--- Score

45. Has a Security Apps requirement not been met?
<--- Score

46. Is Security Apps currently on schedule according to the plan?
<--- Score

47. How are consistent Security Apps definitions important?
<--- Score

48. Is it clearly defined in and to your organization what you do?
<--- Score

49. What would be the goal or target for a Security Apps's improvement team?
<--- Score

50. Is the team formed and are team leaders (Coaches and Management Leads) assigned?
<--- Score

51. Is the current 'as is' process being followed? If not, what are the discrepancies?
<--- Score

52. Has the improvement team collected the 'voice of the customer' (obtained feedback – qualitative and

quantitative)?
<--- Score

53. What are the rough order estimates on cost savings/opportunities that Security Apps brings?
<--- Score

54. Do you all define Security Apps in the same way?
<--- Score

55. What are the Security Apps tasks and definitions?
<--- Score

56. What is out of scope?
<--- Score

57. What is the scope of Security Apps?
<--- Score

58. What Security Apps services do you require?
<--- Score

59. How will variation in the actual durations of each activity be dealt with to ensure that the expected Security Apps results are met?
<--- Score

60. Is the work to date meeting requirements?
<--- Score

61. Has the direction changed at all during the course of Security Apps? If so, when did it change and why?
<--- Score

62. What specifically is the problem? Where does it

occur? When does it occur? What is its extent?
<--- Score

63. What sources do you use to gather information for a Security Apps study?
<--- Score

64. What are the Roles and Responsibilities for each team member and its leadership? Where is this documented?
<--- Score

65. Are roles and responsibilities formally defined?
<--- Score

66. Is special Security Apps user knowledge required?
<--- Score

67. Are there different segments of customers?
<--- Score

68. What is in scope?
<--- Score

69. Are audit criteria, scope, frequency and methods defined?
<--- Score

70. Is Security Apps required?
<--- Score

71. What are (control) requirements for Security Apps Information?
<--- Score

72. What are the record-keeping requirements of

Security Apps activities?
<--- Score

73. What are the dynamics of the communication plan?
<--- Score

74. How do you hand over Security Apps context?
<--- Score

75. What customer feedback methods were used to solicit their input?
<--- Score

76. Is scope creep really all bad news?
<--- Score

77. What critical content must be communicated – who, what, when, where, and how?
<--- Score

78. If substitutes have been appointed, have they been briefed on the Security Apps goals and received regular communications as to the progress to date?
<--- Score

79. Are approval levels defined for contracts and supplements to contracts?
<--- Score

80. Has a team charter been developed and communicated?
<--- Score

81. What intelligence can you gather?
<--- Score

82. What are the boundaries of the scope? What is in bounds and what is not? What is the start point? What is the stop point?
<--- Score

83. What constraints exist that might impact the team?
<--- Score

84. What sort of initial information to gather?
<--- Score

85. Has everyone on the team, including the team leaders, been properly trained?
<--- Score

86. Is the Security Apps scope complete and appropriately sized?
<--- Score

87. Has a project plan, Gantt chart, or similar been developed/completed?
<--- Score

88. Is data collected and displayed to better understand customer(s) critical needs and requirements.
<--- Score

89. How did the Security Apps manager receive input to the development of a Security Apps improvement plan and the estimated completion dates/times of each activity?
<--- Score

90. Is there a completed SIPOC representation, describing the Suppliers, Inputs, Process, Outputs, and Customers?
<--- Score

91. How do you think the partners involved in Security Apps would have defined success?
<--- Score

92. Who is gathering Security Apps information?
<--- Score

93. Are task requirements clearly defined?
<--- Score

94. Have all basic functions of Security Apps been defined?
<--- Score

95. Has/have the customer(s) been identified?
<--- Score

96. How do you keep key subject matter experts in the loop?
<--- Score

97. Are accountability and ownership for Security Apps clearly defined?
<--- Score

98. How was the 'as is' process map developed, reviewed, verified and validated?
<--- Score

99. Have the customer needs been translated into specific, measurable requirements? How?

<--- Score

100. Who are the Security Apps improvement team members, including Management Leads and Coaches?
<--- Score

101. What system do you use for gathering Security Apps information?
<--- Score

102. Is full participation by members in regularly held team meetings guaranteed?
<--- Score

103. How do you manage changes in Security Apps requirements?
<--- Score

104. How do you gather the stories?
<--- Score

105. What are the compelling stakeholder reasons for embarking on Security Apps?
<--- Score

106. Is the scope of Security Apps defined?
<--- Score

107. When is the estimated completion date?
<--- Score

108. Do you have organizational privacy requirements?
<--- Score

109. What information should you gather?
<--- Score

110. Have all of the relationships been defined properly?
<--- Score

111. Is the team sponsored by a champion or stakeholder leader?
<--- Score

112. How would you define the culture at your organization, how susceptible is it to Security Apps changes?
<--- Score

113. What is the scope of the Security Apps effort?
<--- Score

114. Does the scope remain the same?
<--- Score

115. How does the Security Apps manager ensure against scope creep?
<--- Score

116. Is there a critical path to deliver Security Apps results?
<--- Score

117. What scope do you want your strategy to cover?
<--- Score

118. Has a high-level 'as is' process map been completed, verified and validated?

<--- Score

119. Is Security Apps linked to key stakeholder goals and objectives?
<--- Score

120. Is there a clear Security Apps case definition?
<--- Score

121. How do you build the right business case?
<--- Score

122. Are the Security Apps requirements complete?
<--- Score

123. Are there any constraints known that bear on the ability to perform Security Apps work? How is the team addressing them?
<--- Score

124. What is the context?
<--- Score

125. How do you gather requirements?
<--- Score

126. Are customer(s) identified and segmented according to their different needs and requirements?
<--- Score

127. What baselines are required to be defined and managed?
<--- Score

128. Where can you gather more information?
<--- Score

129. What key stakeholder process output measure(s) does Security Apps leverage and how?
<--- Score

130. Is there a Security Apps management charter, including stakeholder case, problem and goal statements, scope, milestones, roles and responsibilities, communication plan?
<--- Score

131. Has anyone else (internal or external to the group) attempted to solve this problem or a similar one before? If so, what knowledge can be leveraged from these previous efforts?
<--- Score

132. What gets examined?
<--- Score

133. What are the requirements for audit information?
<--- Score

134. How have you defined all Security Apps requirements first?
<--- Score

135. What Security Apps requirements should be gathered?
<--- Score

136. Is the team equipped with available and reliable resources?
<--- Score

137. Will team members perform Security Apps work

when assigned and in a timely fashion?
<--- Score

138. What is out-of-scope initially?
<--- Score

139. Why are you doing Security Apps and what is the scope?
<--- Score

140. How often are the team meetings?
<--- Score

141. How can the value of Security Apps be defined?
<--- Score

Add up total points for this section:
_____ = Total points for this section

Divided by: _____ (number of statements answered) = _____
Average score for this section

Transfer your score to the Security Apps Index at the beginning of the Self-Assessment.

CRITERION #3: MEASURE:

INTENT: Gather the correct data.
Measure the current performance and
evolution of the situation.

In my belief, the answer to this
question is clearly defined:

5 Strongly Agree

4 Agree

3 Neutral

2 Disagree

1 Strongly Disagree

1. Do the benefits outweigh the costs?
<--- Score

2. What are the uncertainties surrounding estimates
of impact?
<--- Score

3. What is an unallowable cost?
<--- Score

4. Are Security Apps vulnerabilities categorized and prioritized?
<--- Score

5. Are the Security Apps benefits worth its costs?
<--- Score

6. Have you included everything in your Security Apps cost models?
<--- Score

7. Are there competing Security Apps priorities?
<--- Score

8. How do you verify the Security Apps requirements quality?
<--- Score

9. How is the value delivered by Security Apps being measured?
<--- Score

10. What are your primary costs, revenues, assets?
<--- Score

11. What are the strategic priorities for this year?
<--- Score

12. Was a business case (cost/benefit) developed?
<--- Score

13. Do you have any cost Security Apps limitation requirements?
<--- Score

14. Is the solution cost-effective?

<--- Score

15. Are there measurements based on task performance?

<--- Score

16. How do you measure variability?

<--- Score

17. What is measured? Why?

<--- Score

18. What causes innovation to fail or succeed in your organization?

<--- Score

19. How will your organization measure success?

<--- Score

20. What are the costs?

<--- Score

21. How do you verify your resources?

<--- Score

22. What is the root cause(s) of the problem?

<--- Score

23. Have you made assumptions about the shape of the future, particularly its impact on your customers and competitors?

<--- Score

24. How will costs be allocated?

<--- Score

25. How to cause the change?
<--- Score

26. Do you have an issue in getting priority?
<--- Score

27. How do you verify and validate the Security Apps data?
<--- Score

28. Are you able to realize any cost savings?
<--- Score

29. What can be used to verify compliance?
<--- Score

30. How can you manage cost down?
<--- Score

31. What do you measure and why?
<--- Score

32. Is the cost worth the Security Apps effort ?
<--- Score

33. How are measurements made?
<--- Score

34. What does losing customers cost your organization?
<--- Score

35. What are your key Security Apps organizational performance measures, including key short and longer-term financial measures?

<--- Score

36. Is there an opportunity to verify requirements?
<--- Score

37. What are the types and number of measures to use?
<--- Score

38. What measurements are being captured?
<--- Score

39. What is the total fixed cost?
<--- Score

40. What does your operating model cost?
<--- Score

41. What causes extra work or rework?
<--- Score

42. What is the total cost related to deploying Security Apps, including any consulting or professional services?
<--- Score

43. What are allowable costs?
<--- Score

44. What disadvantage does this cause for the user?
<--- Score

45. What is your Security Apps quality cost segregation study?
<--- Score

46. What evidence is there and what is measured?
<--- Score

47. How do your measurements capture actionable Security Apps information for use in exceeding your customers expectations and securing your customers engagement?
<--- Score

48. How do you measure success?
<--- Score

49. Has a cost center been established?
<--- Score

50. Are the units of measure consistent?
<--- Score

51. How frequently do you track Security Apps measures?
<--- Score

52. What do people want to verify?
<--- Score

53. Where is it measured?
<--- Score

54. Will Security Apps have an impact on current business continuity, disaster recovery processes and/or infrastructure?
<--- Score

55. Which Security Apps impacts are significant?
<--- Score

56. How do you verify and develop ideas and innovations?
<--- Score

57. Are you aware of what could cause a problem?
<--- Score

58. Are indirect costs charged to the Security Apps program?
<--- Score

59. How do you quantify and qualify impacts?
<--- Score

60. Did you tackle the cause or the symptom?
<--- Score

61. Have design-to-cost goals been established?
<--- Score

62. Are you taking your company in the direction of better and revenue or cheaper and cost?
<--- Score

63. What are you verifying?
<--- Score

64. What could cause you to change course?
<--- Score

65. How do you prevent mis-estimating cost?
<--- Score

66. What are the Security Apps investment costs?
<--- Score

67. What are your operating costs?
<--- Score

68. What could cause delays in the schedule?
<--- Score

69. Which costs should be taken into account?
<--- Score

70. How can you reduce costs?
<--- Score

71. What relevant entities could be measured?
<--- Score

72. How do you control the overall costs of your work processes?
<--- Score

73. Do you effectively measure and reward individual and team performance?
<--- Score

74. When are costs are incurred?
<--- Score

75. Why do the measurements/indicators matter?
<--- Score

76. What are the costs of reform?
<--- Score

77. What would be a real cause for concern?
<--- Score

78. How is progress measured?
<--- Score

79. How can a Security Apps test verify your ideas or assumptions?
<--- Score

80. At what cost?
<--- Score

81. What are the Security Apps key cost drivers?
<--- Score

82. What are the costs and benefits?
<--- Score

83. What harm might be caused?
<--- Score

84. Why do you expend time and effort to implement measurement, for whom?
<--- Score

85. Who pays the cost?
<--- Score

86. Where is the cost?
<--- Score

87. How is performance measured?
<--- Score

88. What causes investor action?
<--- Score

89. What would it cost to replace your technology?

<--- Score

90. Do you verify that corrective actions were taken?
<--- Score

91. What causes mismanagement?
<--- Score

92. What drives O&M cost?
<--- Score

93. What methods are feasible and acceptable to estimate the impact of reforms?
<--- Score

94. What tests verify requirements?
<--- Score

95. What details are required of the Security Apps cost structure?
<--- Score

96. What are the operational costs after Security Apps deployment?
<--- Score

97. Do you aggressively reward and promote the people who have the biggest impact on creating excellent Security Apps services/products?
<--- Score

98. Does a Security Apps quantification method exist?
<--- Score

99. Who is involved in verifying compliance?
<--- Score

100. What is the cause of any Security Apps gaps?
<--- Score

101. Are the measurements objective?
<--- Score

102. Are actual costs in line with budgeted costs?
<--- Score

103. How can you reduce the costs of obtaining inputs?
<--- Score

104. How do you aggregate measures across priorities?
<--- Score

105. Do you have a flow diagram of what happens?
<--- Score

106. Are missed Security Apps opportunities costing your organization money?
<--- Score

107. How will you measure your Security Apps effectiveness?
<--- Score

108. Does management have the right priorities among projects?
<--- Score

109. How will effects be measured?
<--- Score

110. What are the costs of delaying Security Apps action?
<--- Score

111. How do you measure lifecycle phases?
<--- Score

112. How do you verify the authenticity of the data and information used?
<--- Score

113. How do you verify if Security Apps is built right?
<--- Score

114. How will success or failure be measured?
<--- Score

115. When should you bother with diagrams?
<--- Score

116. What are the current costs of the Security Apps process?
<--- Score

117. Is it possible to estimate the impact of unanticipated complexity such as wrong or failed assumptions, feedback, etcetera on proposed reforms?
<--- Score

118. How sensitive must the Security Apps strategy be to cost?
<--- Score

119. What potential environmental factors impact the

Security Apps effort?

<--- Score

120. Where can you go to verify the info?

<--- Score

121. What measurements are possible, practicable and meaningful?

<--- Score

122. Among the Security Apps product and service cost to be estimated, which is considered hardest to estimate?

<--- Score

123. How do you verify performance?

<--- Score

124. How do you measure efficient delivery of Security Apps services?

<--- Score

125. How can you measure Security Apps in a systematic way?

<--- Score

126. What are your customers expectations and measures?

<--- Score

127. What are hidden Security Apps quality costs?

<--- Score

128. Does the Security Apps task fit the client's priorities?

<--- Score

129. Who should receive measurement reports?
<--- Score

130. What are the estimated costs of proposed changes?
<--- Score

131. How are costs allocated?
<--- Score

132. What does a Test Case verify?
<--- Score

Add up total points for this section:
_ _ _ _ _ = Total points for this section

Divided by: _ _ _ _ _ _ (number of statements answered) = _ _ _ _ _ _
Average score for this section

Transfer your score to the Security Apps Index at the beginning of the Self-Assessment.

CRITERION #4: ANALYZE:

INTENT: Analyze causes, assumptions and hypotheses.

In my belief, the answer to this question is clearly defined:

5 Strongly Agree

4 Agree

3 Neutral

2 Disagree

1 Strongly Disagree

1. Who qualifies to gain access to data?
<--- Score

2. How is the Security Apps Value Stream Mapping managed?
<--- Score

3. Was a detailed process map created to amplify critical steps of the 'as is' stakeholder process?
<--- Score

4. What output to create?
<--- Score

5. How will corresponding data be collected?
<--- Score

6. What Security Apps data will be collected?
<--- Score

7. Do your leaders quickly bounce back from setbacks?
<--- Score

8. How will the data be checked for quality?
<--- Score

9. What does the data say about the performance of the stakeholder process?
<--- Score

10. What were the financial benefits resulting from any 'ground fruit or low-hanging fruit' (quick fixes)?
<--- Score

11. How do you measure the operational performance of your key work systems and processes, including productivity, cycle time, and other appropriate measures of process effectiveness, efficiency, and innovation?
<--- Score

12. What successful thing are you doing today that may be blinding you to new growth opportunities?
<--- Score

13. What training and qualifications will you need?
<--- Score

14. What conclusions were drawn from the team's data collection and analysis? How did the team reach these conclusions?
<--- Score

15. What are evaluation criteria for the output?
<--- Score

16. Do you, as a leader, bounce back quickly from setbacks?
<--- Score

17. Do staff qualifications match your project?
<--- Score

18. Where is Security Apps data gathered?
<--- Score

19. What were the crucial 'moments of truth' on the process map?
<--- Score

20. Do your contracts/agreements contain data security obligations?
<--- Score

21. Do quality systems drive continuous improvement?
<--- Score

22. How often will data be collected for measures?
<--- Score

23. What are your Security Apps processes?
<--- Score

24. Were Pareto charts (or similar) used to portray the 'heavy hitters' (or key sources of variation)?
<--- Score

25. Do several people in different organizational units assist with the Security Apps process?
<--- Score

26. A compounding model resolution with available relevant data can often provide insight towards a solution methodology; which Security Apps models, tools and techniques are necessary?
<--- Score

27. Who owns what data?
<--- Score

28. How can risk management be tied procedurally to process elements?
<--- Score

29. How does the organization define, manage, and improve its Security Apps processes?
<--- Score

30. Did any value-added analysis or 'lean thinking' take place to identify some of the gaps shown on the 'as is' process map?
<--- Score

31. What is the Value Stream Mapping?
<--- Score

32. Record-keeping requirements flow from the records needed as inputs, outputs, controls and for transformation of a Security Apps process, are the records needed as inputs to the Security Apps process available?

<--- Score

33. What process improvements will be needed?

<--- Score

34. What qualifications do Security Apps leaders need?

<--- Score

35. What are your current levels and trends in key measures or indicators of Security Apps product and process performance that are important to and directly serve your customers? How do these results compare with the performance of your competitors and other organizations with similar offerings?

<--- Score

36. What are your best practices for minimizing Security Apps project risk, while demonstrating incremental value and quick wins throughout the Security Apps project lifecycle?

<--- Score

37. Is there any way to speed up the process?

<--- Score

38. Is there a strict change management process?

<--- Score

39. Who will gather what data?

<--- Score

40. Are your outputs consistent?

<--- Score

41. Think about the functions involved in your Security Apps project, what processes flow from these functions?

<--- Score

42. How do you identify specific Security Apps investment opportunities and emerging trends?

<--- Score

43. Identify an operational issue in your organization, for example, could a particular task be done more quickly or more efficiently by Security Apps?

<--- Score

44. Is the final output clearly identified?

<--- Score

45. Are gaps between current performance and the goal performance identified?

<--- Score

46. What are the Security Apps business drivers?

<--- Score

47. Is the Security Apps process severely broken such that a re-design is necessary?

<--- Score

48. What Security Apps metrics are outputs of the process?

<--- Score

49. Is there an established change management process?
<--- Score

50. What kind of crime could a potential new hire have committed that would not only not disqualify him/her from being hired by your organization, but would actually indicate that he/she might be a particularly good fit?
<--- Score

51. Think about some of the processes you undertake within your organization, which do you own?
<--- Score

52. Is pre-qualification of suppliers carried out?
<--- Score

53. How do you ensure that the Security Apps opportunity is realistic?
<--- Score

54. Where can you get qualified talent today?
<--- Score

55. Is the required Security Apps data gathered?
<--- Score

56. What are the best opportunities for value improvement?
<--- Score

57. What types of data do your Security Apps indicators require?

<--- Score

58. What, related to, Security Apps processes does your organization outsource?
<--- Score

59. What other jobs or tasks affect the performance of the steps in the Security Apps process?
<--- Score

60. What are your current levels and trends in key Security Apps measures or indicators of product and process performance that are important to and directly serve your customers?
<--- Score

61. How do you promote understanding that opportunity for improvement is not criticism of the status quo, or the people who created the status quo?
<--- Score

62. What are the processes for audit reporting and management?
<--- Score

63. What are the revised rough estimates of the financial savings/opportunity for Security Apps improvements?
<--- Score

64. Is the suppliers process defined and controlled?
<--- Score

65. What are the personnel training and qualifications required?

<--- Score

66. How difficult is it to qualify what Security Apps ROI is?
<--- Score

67. Have the problem and goal statements been updated to reflect the additional knowledge gained from the analyze phase?
<--- Score

68. Who is involved in the management review process?
<--- Score

69. Is data and process analysis, root cause analysis and quantifying the gap/opportunity in place?
<--- Score

70. What qualifications are necessary?
<--- Score

71. Who gets your output?
<--- Score

72. What did the team gain from developing a sub-process map?
<--- Score

73. How was the detailed process map generated, verified, and validated?
<--- Score

74. How are outputs preserved and protected?
<--- Score

75. What internal processes need improvement?
<--- Score

76. Do you have the authority to produce the output?
<--- Score

77. What process should you select for improvement?
<--- Score

78. What is the complexity of the output produced?
<--- Score

79. Do your employees have the opportunity to do what they do best everyday?
<--- Score

80. An organizationally feasible system request is one that considers the mission, goals and objectives of the organization, key questions are: is the Security Apps solution request practical and will it solve a problem or take advantage of an opportunity to achieve company goals?
<--- Score

81. What are your key performance measures or indicators and in-process measures for the control and improvement of your Security Apps processes?
<--- Score

82. Can you add value to the current Security Apps decision-making process (largely qualitative) by incorporating uncertainty modeling (more quantitative)?
<--- Score

83. What Security Apps data do you gather or use

now?
<--- Score

84. Did any additional data need to be collected?
<--- Score

85. What do you need to qualify?
<--- Score

86. What qualifications are needed?
<--- Score

87. How do mission and objectives affect the Security Apps processes of your organization?
<--- Score

88. What is the output?
<--- Score

89. How will the Security Apps data be captured?
<--- Score

90. What data do you need to collect?
<--- Score

91. Are all staff in core Security Apps subjects Highly Qualified?
<--- Score

92. How is Security Apps data gathered?
<--- Score

93. How do you define collaboration and team output?
<--- Score

94. Who is involved with workflow mapping?
<--- Score

95. How has the Security Apps data been gathered?
<--- Score

96. What tools were used to generate the list of possible causes?
<--- Score

97. Who will facilitate the team and process?
<--- Score

98. Should you invest in industry-recognized qualifications?
<--- Score

99. How will the change process be managed?
<--- Score

100. Is the performance gap determined?
<--- Score

101. How is the way you as the leader think and process information affecting your organizational culture?
<--- Score

102. Is the gap/opportunity displayed and communicated in financial terms?
<--- Score

103. Has an output goal been set?
<--- Score

104. What qualifies as competition?

<--- Score

105. What is the cost of poor quality as supported by the team's analysis?
<--- Score

106. What are your outputs?
<--- Score

107. What information qualified as important?
<--- Score

108. What is the oversight process?
<--- Score

109. What systems/processes must you excel at?
<--- Score

110. What is your organizations process which leads to recognition of value generation?
<--- Score

111. Have you defined which data is gathered how?
<--- Score

112. Has data output been validated?
<--- Score

113. What quality tools were used to get through the analyze phase?
<--- Score

114. Are Security Apps changes recognized early enough to be approved through the regular process?
<--- Score

115. What methods do you use to gather Security Apps data?

<--- Score

116. What tools were used to narrow the list of possible causes?

<--- Score

117. Do you understand your management processes today?

<--- Score

118. Are all team members qualified for all tasks?

<--- Score

119. What controls do you have in place to protect data?

<--- Score

120. Were there any improvement opportunities identified from the process analysis?

<--- Score

121. Have any additional benefits been identified that will result from closing all or most of the gaps?

<--- Score

122. What qualifications and skills do you need?

<--- Score

123. What will drive Security Apps change?

<--- Score

124. What Security Apps data should be collected?

<--- Score

125. What is the Security Apps Driver?
<--- Score

126. How is data used for program management and improvement?
<--- Score

127. What are the necessary qualifications?
<--- Score

128. What other organizational variables, such as reward systems or communication systems, affect the performance of this Security Apps process?
<--- Score

129. Was a cause-and-effect diagram used to explore the different types of causes (or sources of variation)?
<--- Score

130. How is the data gathered?
<--- Score

131. How do your work systems and key work processes relate to and capitalize on your core competencies?
<--- Score

132. Were any designed experiments used to generate additional insight into the data analysis?
<--- Score

133. What resources go in to get the desired output?
<--- Score

134. Which Security Apps data should be retained?
<--- Score

Add up total points for this section:
_____ = Total points for this section

Divided by: _____ (number of
statements answered) = _____
Average score for this section

Transfer your score to the Security Apps
Index at the beginning of the Self-
Assessment.

CRITERION #5: IMPROVE:

INTENT: Develop a practical solution. Innovate, establish and test the solution and to measure the results.

In my belief, the answer to this question is clearly defined:

5 Strongly Agree

4 Agree

3 Neutral

2 Disagree

1 Strongly Disagree

1. Who are the Security Apps decision-makers?
<--- Score

2. How will you measure the results?
<--- Score

3. Is the Security Apps risk managed?
<--- Score

4. What can you do to improve?
<--- Score

5. Can you identify any significant risks or exposures to Security Apps third- parties (vendors, service providers, alliance partners etc) that concern you?
<--- Score

6. What tools were most useful during the improve phase?
<--- Score

7. How do you manage and improve your Security Apps work systems to deliver customer value and achieve organizational success and sustainability?
<--- Score

8. How can the phases of Security Apps development be identified?
<--- Score

9. What attendant changes will need to be made to ensure that the solution is successful?
<--- Score

10. What are the Security Apps security risks?
<--- Score

11. Is Security Apps documentation maintained?
<--- Score

12. What do you want to improve?
<--- Score

13. What does the 'should be' process map/design look like?

<--- Score

14. To what extent does management recognize Security Apps as a tool to increase the results?
<--- Score

15. How do you define the solutions' scope?
<--- Score

16. In the past few months, what is the smallest change you have made that has had the biggest positive result? What was it about that small change that produced the large return?
<--- Score

17. Are risk triggers captured?
<--- Score

18. How can you improve performance?
<--- Score

19. How risky is your organization?
<--- Score

20. What went well, what should change, what can improve?
<--- Score

21. What tools do you use once you have decided on a Security Apps strategy and more importantly how do you choose?
<--- Score

22. How do you manage Security Apps risk?
<--- Score

23. How risky is your organization?
<--- Score

24. How does the team improve its work?
<--- Score

25. If you could go back in time five years, what decision would you make differently? What is your best guess as to what decision you're making today you might regret five years from now?
<--- Score

26. What needs improvement? Why?
<--- Score

27. Is the Security Apps solution sustainable?
<--- Score

28. Who are the key stakeholders for the Security Apps evaluation?
<--- Score

29. What are the expected Security Apps results?
<--- Score

30. What is the risk?
<--- Score

31. Are the key business and technology risks being managed?
<--- Score

32. Is there a high likelihood that any recommendations will achieve their intended results?
<--- Score

33. How do you decide how much to remunerate an employee?
<--- Score

34. Is the implementation plan designed?
<--- Score

35. What are your current levels and trends in key measures or indicators of workforce and leader development?
<--- Score

36. How do you go about comparing Security Apps approaches/solutions?
<--- Score

37. How will you know that a change is an improvement?
<--- Score

38. Is the scope clearly documented?
<--- Score

39. Is there any other Security Apps solution?
<--- Score

40. Do those selected for the Security Apps team have a good general understanding of what Security Apps is all about?
<--- Score

41. What were the underlying assumptions on the cost-benefit analysis?
<--- Score

42. Can the solution be designed and

implemented within an acceptable time period?
<--- Score

43. Who makes the Security Apps decisions in your organization?
<--- Score

44. Who will be responsible for documenting the Security Apps requirements in detail?
<--- Score

45. Was a Security Apps charter developed?
<--- Score

46. How are policy decisions made and where?
<--- Score

47. What is the magnitude of the improvements?
<--- Score

48. What is Security Apps's impact on utilizing the best solution(s)?
<--- Score

49. Who are the people involved in developing and implementing Security Apps?
<--- Score

50. What were the criteria for evaluating a Security Apps pilot?
<--- Score

51. What error proofing will be done to address some of the discrepancies observed in the 'as is' process?
<--- Score

52. How do you keep improving Security Apps?
<--- Score

53. What are the affordable Security Apps risks?
<--- Score

54. How will you know when its improved?
<--- Score

55. What risks do you need to manage?
<--- Score

56. Does a good decision guarantee a good outcome?
<--- Score

57. What practices helps your organization to develop its capacity to recognize patterns?
<--- Score

58. What actually has to improve and by how much?
<--- Score

59. Have you achieved Security Apps improvements?
<--- Score

60. What area needs the greatest improvement?
<--- Score

61. For estimation problems, how do you develop an estimation statement?
<--- Score

62. Is any Security Apps documentation required?
<--- Score

63. For decision problems, how do you develop a

decision statement?

<--- Score

64. Are risk management tasks balanced centrally and locally?

<--- Score

65. Can you integrate quality management and risk management?

<--- Score

66. Who manages supplier risk management in your organization?

<--- Score

67. Is risk periodically assessed?

<--- Score

68. How does your organization evaluate strategic Security Apps success?

<--- Score

69. Explorations of the frontiers of Security Apps will help you build influence, improve Security Apps, optimize decision making, and sustain change, what is your approach?

<--- Score

70. What lessons, if any, from a pilot were incorporated into the design of the full-scale solution?

<--- Score

71. Is supporting Security Apps documentation required?

<--- Score

72. How can skill-level changes improve Security Apps?
<--- Score

73. How do you link measurement and risk?
<--- Score

74. How can you better manage risk?
<--- Score

75. Is the optimal solution selected based on testing and analysis?
<--- Score

76. Is the solution technically practical?
<--- Score

77. How is continuous improvement applied to risk management?
<--- Score

78. How do you deal with Security Apps risk?
<--- Score

79. Is there a small-scale pilot for proposed improvement(s)? What conclusions were drawn from the outcomes of a pilot?
<--- Score

80. What strategies for Security Apps improvement are successful?
<--- Score

81. Does the goal represent a desired result that can be measured?
<--- Score

82. What resources are required for the improvement efforts?
<--- Score

83. Was a pilot designed for the proposed solution(s)?
<--- Score

84. What to do with the results or outcomes of measurements?
<--- Score

85. Will the controls trigger any other risks?
<--- Score

86. How do you improve your likelihood of success ?
<--- Score

87. Risk factors: what are the characteristics of Security Apps that make it risky?
<--- Score

88. What improvements have been achieved?
<--- Score

89. How significant is the improvement in the eyes of the end user?
<--- Score

90. Is the Security Apps documentation thorough?
<--- Score

91. What is the Security Apps's sustainability risk?
<--- Score

92. Who manages Security Apps risk?

<--- Score

93. When you map the key players in your own work and the types/domains of relationships with them, which relationships do you find easy and which challenging, and why?
<--- Score

94. How do the Security Apps results compare with the performance of your competitors and other organizations with similar offerings?
<--- Score

95. How do you improve Security Apps service perception, and satisfaction?
<--- Score

96. Do you have the optimal project management team structure?
<--- Score

97. Are you assessing Security Apps and risk?
<--- Score

98. Where do you need Security Apps improvement?
<--- Score

99. What current systems have to be understood and/or changed?
<--- Score

100. What are the implications of the one critical Security Apps decision 10 minutes, 10 months, and 10 years from now?
<--- Score

101. What is the team's contingency plan for potential problems occurring in implementation?
<--- Score

102. Do you combine technical expertise with business knowledge and Security Apps Key topics include lifecycles, development approaches, requirements and how to make a business case?
<--- Score

103. What tools were used to tap into the creativity and encourage 'outside the box' thinking?
<--- Score

104. What tools were used to evaluate the potential solutions?
<--- Score

105. Are the risks fully understood, reasonable and manageable?
<--- Score

106. Do you cover the five essential competencies: Communication, Collaboration,Innovation, Adaptability, and Leadership that improve an organizations ability to leverage the new Security Apps in a volatile global economy?
<--- Score

107. How do you measure risk?
<--- Score

108. At what point will vulnerability assessments be performed once Security Apps is put into production (e.g., ongoing Risk Management after

implementation)?

<--- Score

109. What should a proof of concept or pilot accomplish?

<--- Score

110. Who will be using the results of the measurement activities?

<--- Score

111. How scalable is your Security Apps solution?

<--- Score

112. How do you improve productivity?

<--- Score

113. How will you recognize and celebrate results?

<--- Score

114. Are events managed to resolution?

<--- Score

115. What Security Apps improvements can be made?

<--- Score

116. Who do you report Security Apps results to?

<--- Score

117. What is the implementation plan?

<--- Score

118. Risk events: what are the things that could go wrong?

<--- Score

119. Do you need to do a usability evaluation?
<--- Score

120. Are procedures documented for managing Security Apps risks?
<--- Score

121. What are the concrete Security Apps results?
<--- Score

122. What communications are necessary to support the implementation of the solution?
<--- Score

123. Were any criteria developed to assist the team in testing and evaluating potential solutions?
<--- Score

124. Who controls the risk?
<--- Score

125. How do you mitigate Security Apps risk?
<--- Score

126. Who controls key decisions that will be made?
<--- Score

127. Security Apps risk decisions: whose call Is It?
<--- Score

128. Are decisions made in a timely manner?
<--- Score

129. Is there a cost/benefit analysis of optimal solution(s)?
<--- Score

130. Is pilot data collected and analyzed?
<--- Score

131. What is Security Apps risk?
<--- Score

132. Have you identified breakpoints and/or risk tolerances that will trigger broad consideration of a potential need for intervention or modification of strategy?
<--- Score

133. How can you improve Security Apps?
<--- Score

134. Why improve in the first place?
<--- Score

135. Do vendor agreements bring new compliance risk ?
<--- Score

136. Would you develop a Security Apps Communication Strategy?
<--- Score

137. How are Security Apps risks managed?
<--- Score

138. Who will be responsible for making the decisions to include or exclude requested changes once Security Apps is underway?
<--- Score

139. What alternative responses are available to

manage risk?

<--- Score

Add up total points for this section:
_____ = Total points for this section

Divided by: _____ (number of
statements answered) = _____
Average score for this section

Transfer your score to the Security Apps
Index at the beginning of the Self-
Assessment.

CRITERION #6: CONTROL:

INTENT: Implement the practical solution. Maintain the performance and correct possible complications.

In my belief, the answer to this question is clearly defined:

5 Strongly Agree

4 Agree

3 Neutral

2 Disagree

1 Strongly Disagree

1. What key inputs and outputs are being measured on an ongoing basis?
<--- Score

2. Do you monitor the Security Apps decisions made and fine tune them as they evolve?
<--- Score

3. How will the process owner and team be able to

hold the gains?

<--- Score

4. Are operating procedures consistent?

<--- Score

5. Is reporting being used or needed?

<--- Score

6. Is there documentation that will support the successful operation of the improvement?

<--- Score

7. What other systems, operations, processes, and infrastructures (hiring practices, staffing, training, incentives/rewards, metrics/dashboards/scorecards, etc.) need updates, additions, changes, or deletions in order to facilitate knowledge transfer and improvements?

<--- Score

8. How do you establish and deploy modified action plans if circumstances require a shift in plans and rapid execution of new plans?

<--- Score

9. Who is going to spread your message?

<--- Score

10. What do you stand for--and what are you against?

<--- Score

11. What is your theory of human motivation, and how does your compensation plan fit with that view?

<--- Score

12. How will the day-to-day responsibilities for monitoring and continual improvement be transferred from the improvement team to the process owner?
<--- Score

13. Who will be in control?
<--- Score

14. How might the group capture best practices and lessons learned so as to leverage improvements?
<--- Score

15. How will you measure your QA plan's effectiveness?
<--- Score

16. Are the planned controls working?
<--- Score

17. Are suggested corrective/restorative actions indicated on the response plan for known causes to problems that might surface?
<--- Score

18. Has the Security Apps value of standards been quantified?
<--- Score

19. What are you attempting to measure/monitor?
<--- Score

20. Is there a control plan in place for sustaining improvements (short and long-term)?
<--- Score

21. What are the known security controls?
<--- Score

22. What is your plan to assess your security risks?
<--- Score

23. Implementation Planning: is a pilot needed to test the changes before a full roll out occurs?
<--- Score

24. What can you control?
<--- Score

25. Will existing staff require re-training, for example, to learn new business processes?
<--- Score

26. Do the Security Apps decisions you make today help people and the planet tomorrow?
<--- Score

27. Does job training on the documented procedures need to be part of the process team's education and training?
<--- Score

28. Will your goals reflect your program budget?
<--- Score

29. How widespread is its use?
<--- Score

30. How do controls support value?
<--- Score

31. What quality tools were useful in the control

phase?

<--- Score

32. Do you monitor the effectiveness of your Security Apps activities?

<--- Score

33. Will the team be available to assist members in planning investigations?

<--- Score

34. Does Security Apps appropriately measure and monitor risk?

<--- Score

35. Is there a documented and implemented monitoring plan?

<--- Score

36. Are the Security Apps standards challenging?

<--- Score

37. Who controls critical resources?

<--- Score

38. Who has control over resources?

<--- Score

39. Will any special training be provided for results interpretation?

<--- Score

40. What Security Apps standards are applicable?

<--- Score

41. Is there a transfer of ownership and knowledge

to process owner and process team tasked with the responsibilities.
<--- Score

42. Is new knowledge gained imbedded in the response plan?
<--- Score

43. Have new or revised work instructions resulted?
<--- Score

44. Is there a recommended audit plan for routine surveillance inspections of Security Apps's gains?
<--- Score

45. Against what alternative is success being measured?
<--- Score

46. How do you monitor usage and cost?
<--- Score

47. Is there a standardized process?
<--- Score

48. How do your controls stack up?
<--- Score

49. How will Security Apps decisions be made and monitored?
<--- Score

50. Are documented procedures clear and easy to follow for the operators?
<--- Score

51. Are pertinent alerts monitored, analyzed and distributed to appropriate personnel?
<--- Score

52. Is there a Security Apps Communication plan covering who needs to get what information when?
<--- Score

53. What are the critical parameters to watch?
<--- Score

54. What is the standard for acceptable Security Apps performance?
<--- Score

55. You may have created your quality measures at a time when you lacked resources, technology wasn't up to the required standard, or low service levels were the industry norm. Have those circumstances changed?
<--- Score

56. How is change control managed?
<--- Score

57. Are new process steps, standards, and documentation ingrained into normal operations?
<--- Score

58. Has the improved process and its steps been standardized?
<--- Score

59. Does the response plan contain a definite closed loop continual improvement scheme (e.g., plan-do-

check-act)?
<--- Score

60. How likely is the current Security Apps plan to come in on schedule or on budget?
<--- Score

61. Act/Adjust: What Do you Need to Do Differently?
<--- Score

62. What are the key elements of your Security Apps performance improvement system, including your evaluation, organizational learning, and innovation processes?
<--- Score

63. What should you measure to verify efficiency gains?
<--- Score

64. What is the control/monitoring plan?
<--- Score

65. What are customers monitoring?
<--- Score

66. What adjustments to the strategies are needed?
<--- Score

67. What do your reports reflect?
<--- Score

68. How can you best use all of your knowledge repositories to enhance learning and sharing?
<--- Score

69. What are your results for key measures or indicators of the accomplishment of your Security Apps strategy and action plans, including building and strengthening core competencies?
<--- Score

70. Are controls in place and consistently applied?
<--- Score

71. Who sets the Security Apps standards?
<--- Score

72. How will input, process, and output variables be checked to detect for sub-optimal conditions?
<--- Score

73. What do you measure to verify effectiveness gains?
<--- Score

74. How do you encourage people to take control and responsibility?
<--- Score

75. In the case of a Security Apps project, the criteria for the audit derive from implementation objectives, an audit of a Security Apps project involves assessing whether the recommendations outlined for implementation have been met, can you track that any Security Apps project is implemented as planned, and is it working?
<--- Score

76. How do you select, collect, align, and integrate Security Apps data and information for tracking daily operations and overall organizational

performance, including progress relative to strategic objectives and action plans?
<--- Score

77. What should the next improvement project be that is related to Security Apps?
<--- Score

78. Does a troubleshooting guide exist or is it needed?
<--- Score

79. Is knowledge gained on process shared and institutionalized?
<--- Score

80. How will new or emerging customer needs/ requirements be checked/communicated to orient the process toward meeting the new specifications and continually reducing variation?
<--- Score

81. How will the process owner verify improvement in present and future sigma levels, process capabilities?
<--- Score

82. Who is the Security Apps process owner?
<--- Score

83. Does the Security Apps performance meet the customer's requirements?
<--- Score

84. Are the planned controls in place?
<--- Score

85. Is a response plan in place for when the input,

process, or output measures indicate an 'out-of-control' condition?

<--- Score

86. What other areas of the group might benefit from the Security Apps team's improvements, knowledge, and learning?

<--- Score

87. Can support from partners be adjusted?

<--- Score

88. Is a response plan established and deployed?

<--- Score

89. How is Security Apps project cost planned, managed, monitored?

<--- Score

90. Is the Security Apps test/monitoring cost justified?

<--- Score

91. Are there documented procedures?

<--- Score

92. How will report readings be checked to effectively monitor performance?

<--- Score

93. What is the recommended frequency of auditing?

<--- Score

94. Are you measuring, monitoring and predicting Security Apps activities to optimize operations and profitability, and enhancing outcomes?

<--- Score

Add up total points for this section:
_____ = Total points for this section

Divided by: _____ (number of
statements answered) = _____
Average score for this section

Transfer your score to the Security Apps
Index at the beginning of the Self-
Assessment.

CRITERION #7: SUSTAIN:

INTENT: Retain the benefits.

In my belief, the answer to this question is clearly defined:

5 Strongly Agree

4 Agree

3 Neutral

2 Disagree

1 Strongly Disagree

1. What goals did you miss?
<--- Score

2. How do you know if you are successful?
<--- Score

3. What must you excel at?
<--- Score

4. Can you do all this work?
<--- Score

5. If your company went out of business tomorrow, would anyone who doesn't get a paycheck here care?
<--- Score

6. How do you accomplish your long range Security Apps goals?
<--- Score

7. How can you become more high-tech but still be high touch?
<--- Score

8. What stupid rule would you most like to kill?
<--- Score

9. In the past year, what have you done (or could you have done) to increase the accurate perception of your company/brand as ethical and honest?
<--- Score

10. What is the source of the strategies for Security Apps strengthening and reform?
<--- Score

11. How do you make it meaningful in connecting Security Apps with what users do day-to-day?
<--- Score

12. Who do you want your customers to become?
<--- Score

13. What management system can you use to leverage the Security Apps experience, ideas, and concerns of the people closest to the work to be

done?
<--- Score

14. Are you using a design thinking approach and integrating Innovation, Security Apps Experience, and Brand Value?
<--- Score

15. Has implementation been effective in reaching specified objectives so far?
<--- Score

16. If you had to rebuild your organization without any traditional competitive advantages (i.e., no killer technology, promising research, innovative product/ service delivery model, etcetera), how would your people have to approach their work and collaborate together in order to create the necessary conditions for success?
<--- Score

17. How do you proactively clarify deliverables and Security Apps quality expectations?
<--- Score

18. Think of your Security Apps project, what are the main functions?
<--- Score

19. Is there any reason to believe the opposite of my current belief?
<--- Score

20. When information truly is ubiquitous, when reach and connectivity are completely global, when computing resources are infinite, and when a whole

new set of impossibilities are not only possible, but happening, what will that do to your business?
<--- Score

21. What did you miss in the interview for the worst hire you ever made?
<--- Score

22. What was the last experiment you ran?
<--- Score

23. Why should people listen to you?
<--- Score

24. What are the usability implications of Security Apps actions?
<--- Score

25. Which functions and people interact with the supplier and or customer?
<--- Score

26. Are you maintaining a past–present–future perspective throughout the Security Apps discussion?
<--- Score

27. How do you go about securing Security Apps?
<--- Score

28. What is effective Security Apps?
<--- Score

29. What would you recommend your friend do if he/she were facing this dilemma?
<--- Score

30. How do senior leaders deploy your organizations vision and values through your leadership system, to the workforce, to key suppliers and partners, and to customers and other stakeholders, as appropriate?
<--- Score

31. What are current Security Apps paradigms?
<--- Score

32. Do you know what you are doing? And who do you call if you don't?
<--- Score

33. What new services of functionality will be implemented next with Security Apps ?
<--- Score

34. Do you have the right capabilities and capacities?
<--- Score

35. Who is responsible for Security Apps?
<--- Score

36. Will there be any necessary staff changes (redundancies or new hires)?
<--- Score

37. How do you keep records, of what?
<--- Score

38. Which Security Apps goals are the most important?
<--- Score

39. What is the overall talent health of your

organization as a whole at senior levels, and for each organization reporting to a member of the Senior Leadership Team?
<--- Score

40. Is Security Apps dependent on the successful delivery of a current project?
<--- Score

41. Are you making progress, and are you making progress as Security Apps leaders?
<--- Score

42. Have new benefits been realized?
<--- Score

43. What role does communication play in the success or failure of a Security Apps project?
<--- Score

44. What potential megatrends could make your business model obsolete?
<--- Score

45. What have you done to protect your business from competitive encroachment?
<--- Score

46. How do you lead with Security Apps in mind?
<--- Score

47. What Security Apps modifications can you make work for you?
<--- Score

48. Do you say no to customers for no reason?

<--- Score

49. What is the overall business strategy?
<--- Score

50. What knowledge, skills and characteristics mark a good Security Apps project manager?
<--- Score

51. Who are your customers?
<--- Score

52. Why is Security Apps important for you now?
<--- Score

53. Are there any activities that you can take off your to do list?
<--- Score

54. How does Security Apps integrate with other stakeholder initiatives?
<--- Score

55. What business benefits will Security Apps goals deliver if achieved?
<--- Score

56. Who do you think the world wants your organization to be?
<--- Score

57. What is something you believe that nearly no one agrees with you on?
<--- Score

58. Are you paying enough attention to the partners

your company depends on to succeed?
<--- Score

59. What is your formula for success in Security Apps ?
<--- Score

60. What unique value proposition (UVP) do you offer?
<--- Score

61. How can you become the company that would put you out of business?
<--- Score

62. What counts that you are not counting?
<--- Score

63. Is a Security Apps breakthrough on the horizon?
<--- Score

64. What is your competitive advantage?
<--- Score

65. Do you have past Security Apps successes?
<--- Score

66. What Security Apps skills are most important?
<--- Score

67. Who will manage the integration of tools?
<--- Score

68. What is the kind of project structure that would be appropriate for your Security Apps project, should it be formal and complex, or can it be less formal and relatively simple?
<--- Score

69. What could happen if you do not do it?
<--- Score

70. Are you satisfied with your current role? If not, what is missing from it?
<--- Score

71. How do you foster the skills, knowledge, talents, attributes, and characteristics you want to have?
<--- Score

72. Is there a work around that you can use?
<--- Score

73. Who else should you help?
<--- Score

74. How do you listen to customers to obtain actionable information?
<--- Score

75. What are you trying to prove to yourself, and how might it be hijacking your life and business success?
<--- Score

76. Who do we want your customers to become?
<--- Score

77. At what moment would you think; Will I get fired?
<--- Score

78. What are the key enablers to make this Security Apps move?
<--- Score

79. If you do not follow, then how to lead?
<--- Score

80. Who will provide the final approval of Security Apps deliverables?
<--- Score

81. What are the top 3 things at the forefront of your Security Apps agendas for the next 3 years?
<--- Score

82. What may be the consequences for the performance of an organization if all stakeholders are not consulted regarding Security Apps?
<--- Score

83. How do you deal with Security Apps changes?
<--- Score

84. Were lessons learned captured and communicated?
<--- Score

85. Is there any existing Security Apps governance structure?
<--- Score

86. Can the schedule be done in the given time?
<--- Score

87. Why do and why don't your customers like your organization?
<--- Score

88. What are your personal philosophies regarding Security Apps and how do they influence your work?

<--- Score

89. Who is responsible for errors?
<--- Score

90. Do you see more potential in people than they do in themselves?
<--- Score

91. What happens at your organization when people fail?
<--- Score

92. What is the big Security Apps idea?
<--- Score

93. Who uses your product in ways you never expected?
<--- Score

94. What is it like to work for you?
<--- Score

95. How do you provide a safe environment -physically and emotionally?
<--- Score

96. How long will it take to change?
<--- Score

97. Why will customers want to buy your organizations products/services?
<--- Score

98. How do you set Security Apps stretch targets and how do you get people to not only participate in

setting these stretch targets but also that they strive to achieve these?

<--- Score

99. Who will be responsible for deciding whether Security Apps goes ahead or not after the initial investigations?

<--- Score

100. Will it be accepted by users?

<--- Score

101. How do you track customer value, profitability or financial return, organizational success, and sustainability?

<--- Score

102. Why not do Security Apps?

<--- Score

103. What should you stop doing?

<--- Score

104. What happens when a new employee joins the organization?

<--- Score

105. Whose voice (department, ethnic group, women, older workers, etc) might you have missed hearing from in your company, and how might you amplify this voice to create positive momentum for your business?

<--- Score

106. How will you motivate the stakeholders with the least vested interest?

<--- Score

107. Did your employees make progress today?
<--- Score

108. What one word do you want to own in the minds of your customers, employees, and partners?
<--- Score

109. To whom do you add value?
<--- Score

110. What are the challenges?
<--- Score

111. Are you changing as fast as the world around you?
<--- Score

112. Which individuals, teams or departments will be involved in Security Apps?
<--- Score

113. Do you know who is a friend or a foe?
<--- Score

114. What are the potential basics of Security Apps fraud?
<--- Score

115. Is it economical; do you have the time and money?
<--- Score

116. Who, on the executive team or the board, has

spoken to a customer recently?

<--- Score

117. What are internal and external Security Apps relations?

<--- Score

118. Are you / should you be revolutionary or evolutionary?

<--- Score

119. Is a Security Apps team work effort in place?

<--- Score

120. What is a feasible sequencing of reform initiatives over time?

<--- Score

121. What is an unauthorized commitment?

<--- Score

122. In retrospect, of the projects that you pulled the plug on, what percent do you wish had been allowed to keep going, and what percent do you wish had ended earlier?

<--- Score

123. Is the Security Apps organization completing tasks effectively and efficiently?

<--- Score

124. How do you foster innovation?

<--- Score

125. What does your signature ensure?

<--- Score

126. Ask yourself: how would you do this work if you only had one staff member to do it?
<--- Score

127. Which models, tools and techniques are necessary?
<--- Score

128. How can you incorporate support to ensure safe and effective use of Security Apps into the services that you provide?
<--- Score

129. Can you maintain your growth without detracting from the factors that have contributed to your success?
<--- Score

130. Who are four people whose careers you have enhanced?
<--- Score

131. Who will determine interim and final deadlines?
<--- Score

132. How are you doing compared to your industry?
<--- Score

133. How will you ensure you get what you expected?
<--- Score

134. Are you relevant? Will you be relevant five years from now? Ten?
<--- Score

135. Who is responsible for ensuring appropriate resources (time, people and money) are allocated to Security Apps?
<--- Score

136. Instead of going to current contacts for new ideas, what if you reconnected with dormant contacts--the people you used to know? If you were going reactivate a dormant tie, who would it be?
<--- Score

137. What is your BATNA (best alternative to a negotiated agreement)?
<--- Score

138. Are new benefits received and understood?
<--- Score

139. Where can you break convention?
<--- Score

140. Is your strategy driving your strategy? Or is the way in which you allocate resources driving your strategy?
<--- Score

141. What are the long-term Security Apps goals?
<--- Score

142. What have been your experiences in defining long range Security Apps goals?
<--- Score

143. What is the recommended frequency of auditing?

<--- Score

144. How is implementation research currently incorporated into each of your goals?
<--- Score

145. Are your responses positive or negative?
<--- Score

146. Are the assumptions believable and achievable?
<--- Score

147. How do you govern and fulfill your societal responsibilities?
<--- Score

148. Who have you, as a company, historically been when you've been at your best?
<--- Score

149. How important is Security Apps to the user organizations mission?
<--- Score

150. What trouble can you get into?
<--- Score

151. How do you stay inspired?
<--- Score

152. How do you engage the workforce, in addition to satisfying them?
<--- Score

153. What are specific Security Apps rules to follow?

<--- Score

154. Do you have an implicit bias for capital investments over people investments?
<--- Score

155. What are the performance and scale of the Security Apps tools?
<--- Score

156. Do you feel that more should be done in the Security Apps area?
<--- Score

157. What is your Security Apps strategy?
<--- Score

158. Are assumptions made in Security Apps stated explicitly?
<--- Score

159. What happens if you do not have enough funding?
<--- Score

160. What is the craziest thing you can do?
<--- Score

161. Are all key stakeholders present at all Structured Walkthroughs?
<--- Score

162. How do you determine the key elements that affect Security Apps workforce satisfaction, how are these elements determined for different workforce groups and segments?

<--- Score

163. What do we do when new problems arise?
<--- Score

164. What are the essentials of internal Security Apps management?
<--- Score

165. What is the range of capabilities?
<--- Score

166. What threat is Security Apps addressing?
<--- Score

167. Who are the key stakeholders?
<--- Score

168. Can you break it down?
<--- Score

169. If your customer were your grandmother, would you tell her to buy what you're selling?
<--- Score

170. How do you cross-sell and up-sell your Security Apps success?
<--- Score

171. What trophy do you want on your mantle?
<--- Score

172. How can you negotiate Security Apps successfully with a stubborn boss, an irate client, or a deceitful coworker?
<--- Score

173. What is the purpose of Security Apps in relation to the mission?
<--- Score

174. If you find that you havent accomplished one of the goals for one of the steps of the Security Apps strategy, what will you do to fix it?
<--- Score

175. Whom among your colleagues do you trust, and for what?
<--- Score

176. If no one would ever find out about your accomplishments, how would you lead differently?
<--- Score

177. What is the funding source for this project?
<--- Score

178. Have benefits been optimized with all key stakeholders?
<--- Score

179. Why is it important to have senior management support for a Security Apps project?
<--- Score

180. Why should you adopt a Security Apps framework?
<--- Score

181. How likely is it that a customer would recommend your company to a friend or colleague?
<--- Score

182. Do you have the right people on the bus?
<--- Score

183. How do you create buy-in?
<--- Score

184. What are the success criteria that will indicate that Security Apps objectives have been met and the benefits delivered?
<--- Score

185. What are your most important goals for the strategic Security Apps objectives?
<--- Score

186. Would you rather sell to knowledgeable and informed customers or to uninformed customers?
<--- Score

187. Is the impact that Security Apps has shown?
<--- Score

188. Do you think Security Apps accomplishes the goals you expect it to accomplish?
<--- Score

189. What are the barriers to increased Security Apps production?
<--- Score

190. Are the criteria for selecting recommendations stated?
<--- Score

191. How do customers see your organization?

<--- Score

192. Do you think you know, or do you know you know ?
<--- Score

193. How do you assess the Security Apps pitfalls that are inherent in implementing it?
<--- Score

194. If you were responsible for initiating and implementing major changes in your organization, what steps might you take to ensure acceptance of those changes?
<--- Score

195. How do you transition from the baseline to the target?
<--- Score

196. What are the business goals Security Apps is aiming to achieve?
<--- Score

197. Operational - will it work?
<--- Score

198. How do you keep the momentum going?
<--- Score

199. How do you maintain Security Apps's Integrity?
<--- Score

200. What you are going to do to affect the numbers?
<--- Score

201. If you weren't already in this business, would you enter it today? And if not, what are you going to do about it?
<--- Score

202. Marketing budgets are tighter, consumers are more skeptical, and social media has changed forever the way we talk about Security Apps, how do you gain traction?
<--- Score

203. Who is the main stakeholder, with ultimate responsibility for driving Security Apps forward?
<--- Score

204. Is maximizing Security Apps protection the same as minimizing Security Apps loss?
<--- Score

205. What are strategies for increasing support and reducing opposition?
<--- Score

206. Political -is anyone trying to undermine this project?
<--- Score

207. How do you ensure that implementations of Security Apps products are done in a way that ensures safety?
<--- Score

208. What would have to be true for the option on the table to be the best possible choice?
<--- Score

209. What are the gaps in your knowledge and experience?

<--- Score

210. How much contingency will be available in the budget?

<--- Score

211. How do you manage Security Apps Knowledge Management (KM)?

<--- Score

212. How much does Security Apps help?

<--- Score

213. What is your question? Why?

<--- Score

214. Is your basic point _____ or _____?

<--- Score

215. How will you insure seamless interoperability of Security Apps moving forward?

<--- Score

216. What are the short and long-term Security Apps goals?

<--- Score

217. Do Security Apps rules make a reasonable demand on a users capabilities?

<--- Score

218. What projects are going on in the organization today, and what resources are those projects using

from the resource pools?
<--- Score

219. If there were zero limitations, what would you do differently?
<--- Score

220. How will you know that the Security Apps project has been successful?
<--- Score

Add up total points for this section:
_ _ _ _ _ = Total points for this section

Divided by: _ _ _ _ _ _ (number of statements answered) = _ _ _ _ _ _
Average score for this section

Transfer your score to the Security Apps Index at the beginning of the Self-Assessment.

Security Apps and Managing Projects, Criteria for Project Managers:

1.0 Initiating Process Group: Security Apps

1. What business situation is being addressed?

2. First of all, should any action be taken?

3. Are you properly tracking the progress of the Security Apps project and communicating the status to stakeholders?

4. Does the Security Apps project team have enough people to execute the Security Apps project plan?

5. What were the challenges that you encountered during the execution of a previous Security Apps project that you would not want to repeat?

6. How well did you do?

7. Who is funding the Security Apps project?

8. Did you use a contractor or vendor?

9. Professionals want to know what is expected from them what are the deliverables?

10. What were things that you did well, and could improve, and how?

11. Are the changes in your Security Apps project being formally requested, analyzed, and approved by the appropriate decision makers?

12. Mitigate. what will you do to minimize the impact

should the risk event occur?

13. What do they need to know about the Security Apps project?

14. Were decisions made in a timely manner?

15. If action is called for, what form should it take?

16. Which six sigma dmaic phase focuses on why and how defects and errors occur?

17. What input will you be required to provide the Security Apps project team?

18. Who are the Security Apps project stakeholders?

19. In which Security Apps project management process group is the detailed Security Apps project budget created?

20. Who is behind the Security Apps project?

1.1 Project Charter: Security Apps

21. Why is it important?

22. Strategic fit: what is the strategic initiative identifier for this Security Apps project?

23. Security Apps project deliverables: what is the Security Apps project going to produce?

24. How much?

25. What are the assumptions?

26. Run it as as a startup?

27. Who is the Security Apps project Manager?

28. For whom?

29. What is the purpose of the Security Apps project?

30. What are the deliverables?

31. What date will the task finish?

32. Does the Security Apps project need to consider any special capacity or capability issues?

33. Will this replace an existing product?

34. What is the most common tool for helping define the detail?

35. What are some examples of a business case?

36. Where does all this information come from?

37. How do you manage integration?

38. Must Have?

39. What outcome, in measureable terms, are you hoping to accomplish?

40. Customer: who are you doing the Security Apps project for?

1.2 Stakeholder Register: Security Apps

41. Is your organization ready for change?

42. Who are the stakeholders?

43. How should employers make voices heard?

44. How big is the gap?

45. How much influence do they have on the Security Apps project?

46. What are the major Security Apps project milestones requiring communications or providing communications opportunities?

47. What opportunities exist to provide communications?

48. Who wants to talk about Security?

49. Who is managing stakeholder engagement?

50. How will reports be created?

51. What is the power of the stakeholder?

52. What & Why?

1.3 Stakeholder Analysis Matrix: Security Apps

53. What is your organizations competitors doing?

54. Innovative aspects?

55. Who has control over whom?

56. Experience, knowledge, data?

57. What can the Security Apps projects outcome be used for?

58. Lack of competitive strength?

59. What resources might the stakeholder bring to the Security Apps project?

60. If you can not fix it, how do you do it differently?

61. Arena: in what fields are the actors active, where are they present?

62. Who will be affected by the work?

63. Volumes, production, economies?

64. Is there a clear description of the scope of practice of the Security Apps projects educators?

65. Gaps in capabilities?

66. Reputation, presence and reach?

67. Who is most dependent on the resources at stake?

68. Who are potential allies and opponents?

69. Who is most interested in information about the topic and/or has previously initiated interest?

70. Vulnerable groups; who are the vulnerable groups that might be affected by the Security Apps project?

71. Who will obstruct/hinder the Security Apps project if they are not involved?

72. Supporters; who are the supporters?

2.0 Planning Process Group: Security Apps

73. To what extent have public/private national resources and/or counterparts been mobilized to contribute to the programs objective and produce results and impacts?

74. To what extent and in what ways are the Security Apps project contributing to progress towards organizational reform?

75. Is the pace of implementing the products of the program ensuring the completeness of the results of the Security Apps project?

76. If you are late, will anybody notice?

77. What will you do?

78. To what extent has the intervention strategy been adapted to the areas of intervention in which it is being implemented?

79. What input will you be required to provide the Security Apps project team?

80. Does it make any difference if you are successful?

81. In what way has the program contributed towards the issue culture and development included on the public agenda?

82. How will you do it?

83. Product breakdown structure (pbs): what is the Security Apps project result or product, and how should it look like, what are its parts?

84. In what way has the Security Apps project come up with innovative measures for problem-solving?

85. Are you just doing busywork to pass the time?

86. Have operating capacities been created and/or reinforced in partners?

87. Who are the Security Apps project stakeholders?

88. What is the critical path for this Security Apps project, and what is the duration of the critical path?

89. To what extent do the intervention objectives and strategies of the Security Apps project respond to your organizations plans?

90. When developing the estimates for Security Apps project phases, you choose to add the individual estimates for the activities that comprise each phase. What type of estimation method are you using?

91. Are the necessary foundations in place to ensure the sustainability of the results of the Security Apps project?

2.1 Project Management Plan: Security Apps

92. Will you add a schedule and diagram?

93. Is the budget realistic?

94. What should you drop in order to add something new?

95. What are the training needs?

96. Do the proposed changes from the Security Apps project include any significant risks to safety?

97. What are the assigned resources?

98. How well are you able to manage your risk?

99. Did the planning effort collaborate to develop solutions that integrate expertise, policies, programs, and Security Apps projects across entities?

100. What if, for example, the positive direction and vision of your organization causes expected trends to change resulting in greater need than expected?

101. Are cost risk analysis methods applied to develop contingencies for the estimated total Security Apps project costs?

102. What did not work so well?

103. Is the appropriate plan selected based on your organizations objectives and evaluation criteria expressed in Principles and Guidelines policies?

104. Is mitigation authorized or recommended?

105. Are the existing and future without-plan conditions reasonable and appropriate?

106. Who manages integration?

107. Who is the Security Apps project Manager?

108. When is a Security Apps project management plan created?

109. How can you best help your organization to develop consistent practices in Security Apps project management planning stages?

110. Are there any scope changes proposed for a previously authorized Security Apps project?

2.2 Scope Management Plan: Security Apps

111. Are stakeholders aware and supportive of the principles and practices of modern software estimation?

112. Are meeting minutes captured and sent out after the meeting?

113. Are the people assigned to the Security Apps project sufficiently qualified?

114. What happens if scope changes?

115. Are internal Security Apps project status meetings held at reasonable intervals?

116. Is the Security Apps project status reviewed with the steering and executive teams at appropriate intervals?

117. Are procurement deliverables arriving on time and to specification?

118. Is there a formal set of procedures supporting Stakeholder Management?

119. Have the scope, objectives, costs, benefits and impacts been communicated to all involved and/or impacted stakeholders and work groups?

120. Are meeting objectives identified for each

meeting?

121. Has the Security Apps project scope been baselined?

122. Is it standard practice to formally commit stakeholders to the Security Apps project via agreements?

123. Which statement about customer expectations is not true?

124. Does the implementation plan have an appropriate division of responsibilities?

125. Is an industry recognized mechanized support tool(s) being used for Security Apps project scheduling & tracking?

126. Alignment to strategic goals & objectives?

127. Has the budget been baselined?

128. Are software metrics formally captured, analyzed and used as a basis for other Security Apps project estimates?

129. When will scope verification be performed?

130. Without-plan conditions?

2.3 Requirements Management Plan: Security Apps

131. Have stakeholders been instructed in the Change Control process?

132. To see if a requirement statement is sufficiently well-defined, read it from the developers perspective. Mentally add the phrase, call me when youre done to the end of the requirement and see if that makes you nervous. In other words, would you need additional clarification from the author to understand the requirement well enough to design and implement it?

133. Do you have an agreed upon process for alerting the Security Apps project Manager if a request for change in requirements leads to a product scope change?

134. Who is responsible for quantifying the Security Apps project requirements?

135. Do you really need to write this document at all?

136. Are actual resources expenditures versus planned expenditures acceptable?

137. What cost metrics will be used?

138. How will you develop the schedule of requirements activities?

139. Is the change control process documented?

140. Are all the stakeholders ready for the transition into the user community?

141. Do you know which stakeholders will participate in the requirements effort?

142. Controlling Security Apps project requirements involves monitoring the status of the Security Apps project requirements and managing changes to the requirements. Who is responsible for monitoring and tracking the Security Apps project requirements?

143. Could inaccurate or incomplete requirements in this Security Apps project create a serious risk for the business?

144. How detailed should the Security Apps project get?

145. Who will finally present the work or product(s) for acceptance?

146. After the requirements are gathered and set forth on the requirements register, theyre little more than a laundry list of items. Some may be duplicates, some might conflict with others and some will be too broad or too vague to understand. Describe how the requirements will be analyzed. Who will perform the analysis?

147. Has the requirements team been instructed in the Change Control process?

148. The wbs is developed as part of a joint planning session. and how do you know that youhave done this

right?

149. Did you provide clear and concise specifications?

150. How will the information be distributed?

2.4 Requirements Documentation: Security Apps

151. What can tools do for us?

152. What images does it conjure?

153. Can the requirement be changed without a large impact on other requirements?

154. Where are business rules being captured?

155. How will requirements be documented and who signs off on them?

156. Who is interacting with the system?

157. Is your business case still valid?

158. How does what is being described meet the business need?

159. What are the acceptance criteria?

160. Does the system provide the functions which best support the customers needs?

161. Verifiability. can the requirements be checked?

162. What are current process problems?

163. What variations exist for a process?

164. If applicable; are there issues linked with the fact that this is an offshore Security Apps project?

165. How much testing do you need to do to prove that your system is safe?

166. Validity. does the system provide the functions which best support the customers needs?

167. Can you check system requirements?

168. How does the proposed Security Apps project contribute to the overall objectives of your organization?

169. Is the requirement realistically testable?

2.5 Requirements Traceability Matrix: Security Apps

170. How do you manage scope?

171. How small is small enough?

172. What are the chronologies, contingencies, consequences, criteria?

173. What percentage of Security Apps projects are producing traceability matrices between requirements and other work products?

174. Do you have a clear understanding of all subcontracts in place?

175. Will you use a Requirements Traceability Matrix?

176. Describe the process for approving requirements so they can be added to the traceability matrix and Security Apps project work can be performed. Will the Security Apps project requirements become approved in writing?

177. Is there a requirements traceability process in place?

178. What is the WBS?

179. How will it affect the stakeholders personally in career?

180. Why do you manage scope?

181. Why use a WBS?

2.6 Project Scope Statement: Security Apps

182. What went wrong?

183. Have the reports to be produced, distributed, and filed been defined?

184. Is your organization structure appropriate for the Security Apps projects size and complexity?

185. Did your Security Apps project ask for this?

186. Were potential customers involved early in the planning process?

187. Will all tasks resulting from issues be entered into the Security Apps project Plan and tracked through the plan?

188. Will the qa related information be reported regularly as part of the status reporting mechanisms?

189. Is an issue management process documented and filed?

190. If there is an independent oversight contractor, have they signed off on the Security Apps project Plan?

191. Has the Security Apps project scope statement been reviewed as part of the baseline process?

192. Are the input requirements from the team members clearly documented and communicated?

193. Elements that deal with providing the detail?

194. Is the plan for your organization of the Security Apps project resources adequate?

195. Once its defined, what is the stability of the Security Apps project scope?

196. Does the scope statement still need some clarity?

197. How will you verify the accuracy of the work of the Security Apps project, and what constitutes acceptance of the deliverables?

198. Will this process be communicated to the customer and Security Apps project team?

199. What actions will be taken to mitigate the risk?

200. Any new risks introduced or old risks impacted. Are there issues that could affect the existing requirements for the result, service, or product if the scope changes?

201. Are there adequate Security Apps project control systems?

2.7 Assumption and Constraint Log: Security Apps

202. What do you audit?

203. Does the system design reflect the requirements?

204. Are you meeting your customers expectations consistently?

205. Violation trace: why ?

206. Are formal code reviews conducted?

207. How many Security Apps project staff does this specific process affect?

208. What weaknesses do you have?

209. Have you eliminated all duplicative tasks or manual efforts, where appropriate?

210. How are new requirements or changes to requirements identified?

211. What worked well?

212. Are processes for release management of new development from coding and unit testing, to integration testing, to training, and production defined and followed?

213. What do you log?

214. Contradictory information between different documents?

215. No superfluous information or marketing narrative?

216. Is the steering committee active in Security Apps project oversight?

217. How can constraints be violated?

218. How relevant is this attribute to this Security Apps project or audit?

219. Do the requirements meet the standards of correctness, completeness, consistency, accuracy, and readability?

220. Are there processes in place to ensure internal consistency between the source code components?

221. What is positive about the current process?

2.8 Work Breakdown Structure: Security Apps

222. Why is it useful?

223. What has to be done?

224. How will you and your Security Apps project team define the Security Apps projects scope and work breakdown structure?

225. Do you need another level?

226. Who has to do it?

227. Where does it take place?

228. Is the work breakdown structure (wbs) defined and is the scope of the Security Apps project clear with assigned deliverable owners?

229. How big is a work-package?

230. How far down?

231. When do you stop?

232. When does it have to be done?

233. Is it a change in scope?

234. What is the probability that the Security Apps project duration will exceed xx weeks?

235. How much detail?

236. Can you make it?

237. What is the probability of completing the Security Apps project in less that xx days?

2.9 WBS Dictionary: Security Apps

238. Are records maintained to show how management reserves are used?

239. Do procedures specify under what circumstances replanning of open work packages may occur, and the methods to be followed?

240. Are data elements reconcilable between internal summary reports and reports forwarded to us?

241. Is work progressively subdivided into detailed work packages as requirements are defined?

242. Are overhead cost budgets (or Security Apps projections) established on a facility-wide basis at least annually for the life of the contract?

243. Are records maintained to show full accountability for all material purchased for the contract, including the residual inventory?

244. Identify potential or actual overruns and underruns?

245. Are indirect costs accumulated for comparison with the corresponding budgets?

246. Are current work performance indicators and goals relatable to original goals as modified by contractual changes, replanning, and reprogramming actions?

247. What went right?

248. Is authorization of budgets in excess of the contract budget base controlled formally and done with the full knowledge and recognition of the procuring activity?

249. Evaluate the performance of operating organizations?

250. Is all contract work included in the CWBS?

251. Budgets assigned to control accounts?

252. Does the contractors system description or procedures require that the performance measurement baseline plus management reserve equal the contract budget base?

253. Are estimates developed by Security Apps project personnel coordinated with the already stated responsible for overall management to determine whether required resources will be available according to revised planning?

254. Do the lines of authority for incurring indirect costs correspond to the lines of responsibility for management control of the same components of costs?

255. Does the contractors system include procedures for measuring performance of the lowest level organization responsible for the control account?

2.10 Schedule Management Plan: Security Apps

256. Is there an issues management plan in place?

257. Identify the amount of schedule variation that triggers a warning. What happens if a warning is triggered?

258. Are trade-offs between accepting the risk and mitigating the risk identified?

259. Is current scope of the Security Apps project substantially different than that originally defined?

260. Are updated Security Apps project time & resource estimates reasonable based on the current Security Apps project stage?

261. Is stakeholder involvement adequate?

262. Does the detailed work plan match the complexity of tasks with the capabilities of personnel?

263. Has the schedule been baselined?

264. Are internal Security Apps project status meetings held at reasonable intervals?

265. Does the ims reflect accurate current status and credible start/finish forecasts for all to-go tasks and milestones?

266. Are all activities logically sequenced?

267. Have the key functions and capabilities been defined and assigned to each release or iteration?

268. Are risk triggers captured?

269. Have key stakeholders been identified?

270. Are all key components of a Quality Assurance Plan present?

271. Are mitigation strategies identified?

272. Are Security Apps project leaders committed to this Security Apps project full time?

273. Is the assigned Security Apps project manager a PMP (Certified Security Apps project manager) and experienced?

274. Are post milestone Security Apps project reviews (PMPR) conducted with your organization at least once a year?

275. Has the Security Apps project manager been identified?

2.11 Activity List: Security Apps

276. What did not go as well?

277. What is the probability the Security Apps project can be completed in xx weeks?

278. What went well?

279. For other activities, how much delay can be tolerated?

280. What are you counting on?

281. How should ongoing costs be monitored to try to keep the Security Apps project within budget?

282. How much slack is available in the Security Apps project?

283. Is there anything planned that does not need to be here?

284. When will the work be performed?

285. What are the critical bottleneck activities?

286. When do the individual activities need to start and finish?

287. What is the total time required to complete the Security Apps project if no delays occur?

288. Is infrastructure setup part of your Security Apps

project?

289. What will be performed?

290. Should you include sub-activities?

291. How will it be performed?

292. Who will perform the work?

293. Are the required resources available or need to be acquired?

2.12 Activity Attributes: Security Apps

294. Can you re-assign any activities to another resource to resolve an over-allocation?

295. What is the general pattern here?

296. How difficult will it be to complete specific activities on this Security Apps project?

297. Time for overtime?

298. Resource is assigned to?

299. Have you identified the Activity Leveling Priority code value on each activity?

300. How many days do you need to complete the work scope with a limit of X number of resources?

301. How much activity detail is required?

302. Are the required resources available?

303. How difficult will it be to do specific activities on this Security Apps project?

304. Is there a trend during the year?

305. How many resources do you need to complete the work scope within a limit of X number of days?

306. Where else does it apply?

307. Why?

308. What is missing?

309. How do you manage time?

2.13 Milestone List: Security Apps

310. Effects on core activities, distraction?

311. How soon can the activity start?

312. Information and research?

313. Which path is the critical path?

314. It is to be a narrative text providing the crucial aspects of your Security Apps project proposal answering what, who, how, when and where?

315. Reliability of data, plan predictability?

316. Legislative effects?

317. What are your competitors vulnerabilities?

318. Describe the industry you are in and the market growth opportunities. What is the market for your technology, product or service?

319. Who will manage the Security Apps project on a day-to-day basis?

320. Identify critical paths (one or more) and which activities are on the critical path?

321. Sustaining internal capabilities?

322. Calculate how long can activity be delayed?

323. Obstacles faced?

324. How late can the activity finish?

325. Competitive advantages?

326. Marketing - reach, distribution, awareness?

327. Describe the concept of the technology, product or service that will be or has been developed. How will it be used?

2.14 Network Diagram: Security Apps

328. Why must you schedule milestones, such as reviews, throughout the Security Apps project?

329. Where do you schedule uncertainty time?

330. Where do schedules come from?

331. What is the lowest cost to complete this Security Apps project in xx weeks?

332. Can you calculate the confidence level?

333. What controls the start and finish of a job?

334. Which type of network diagram allows you to depict four types of dependencies?

335. If a current contract exists, can you provide the vendor name, contract start, and contract expiration date?

336. Exercise: what is the probability that the Security Apps project duration will exceed xx weeks?

337. Are you on time?

338. How confident can you be in your milestone dates and the delivery date?

339. If the Security Apps project network diagram cannot change and you have extra personnel resources, what is the BEST thing to do?

340. What can be done concurrently?

341. What is the completion time?

342. What job or jobs precede it?

343. Will crashing x weeks return more in benefits than it costs?

344. What activities must follow this activity?

345. What job or jobs follow it?

346. What is your organizations history in doing similar activities?

2.15 Activity Resource Requirements: Security Apps

347. What are constraints that you might find during the Human Resource Planning process?

348. Other support in specific areas?

349. Are there unresolved issues that need to be addressed?

350. Which logical relationship does the PDM use most often?

351. When does monitoring begin?

352. How do you handle petty cash?

353. Why do you do that?

354. Organizational Applicability?

355. Anything else?

356. Do you use tools like decomposition and rolling-wave planning to produce the activity list and other outputs?

357. What is the Work Plan Standard?

358. How many signatures do you require on a check and does this match what is in your policy and procedures?

2.16 Resource Breakdown Structure: Security Apps

359. What can you do to improve productivity?

360. Any changes from stakeholders?

361. Goals for the Security Apps project. What is each stakeholders desired outcome for the Security Apps project?

362. How should the information be delivered?

363. What defines a successful Security Apps project?

364. Why time management?

365. Who will use the system?

366. Who needs what information?

367. Which resource planning tool provides information on resource responsibility and accountability?

368. Which resources should be in the resource pool?

369. Why do you do it?

370. Changes based on input from stakeholders?

371. Who is allowed to see what data about which resources?

372. Who is allowed to perform which functions?

2.17 Activity Duration Estimates: Security Apps

373. Are procedures defined by which the Security Apps project scope may be changed?

374. Does the case present a realistic scenario?

375. Are activity duration estimates documented?

376. Which would be the NEXT thing for the Security Apps project manager to do?

377. Is training acquired to enhance the skills, knowledge and capabilities of the Security Apps project team?

378. Will additional funds be needed for hardware or software?

379. Are inspections completed to determine if the results comply with the requirements?

380. Is a provider selected based upon defined evaluation criteria?

381. Which is the BEST Security Apps project management tool to use to determine the longest time the Security Apps project will take?

382. Does a process exist to determine the probability of risk events?

383. Does a process exist to formally recognize new Security Apps projects?

384. What is the duration of a milestone?

385. Why is there a new or renewed interest in the field of Security Apps project management?

386. Does a procedure exist to ensure the Security Apps project work is completed in the appropriate sequence and on time?

387. How does the job market and current state of the economy affect human resource management?

388. What tasks must follow this task?

389. Is a standard form used to obtain bids and proposals from prospective sellers?

390. When a risk event occurs, is the risk response evaluated and the appropriate response implemented?

2.18 Duration Estimating Worksheet: Security Apps

391. How can the Security Apps project be displayed graphically to better visualize the activities?

392. Value pocket identification & quantification what are value pockets?

393. Is a construction detail attached (to aid in explanation)?

394. Do any colleagues have experience with your organization and/or RFPs?

395. Done before proceeding with this activity or what can be done concurrently?

396. Can the Security Apps project be constructed as planned?

397. When does your organization expect to be able to complete it?

398. What info is needed?

399. Is this operation cost effective?

400. Will the Security Apps project collaborate with the local community and leverage resources?

401. What work will be included in the Security Apps project?

402. Science = process: remember the scientific method?

403. What is your role?

404. What utility impacts are there?

405. Small or large Security Apps project?

406. How should ongoing costs be monitored to try to keep the Security Apps project within budget?

407. Is the Security Apps project responsive to community need?

2.19 Project Schedule: Security Apps

408. How many levels?

409. Is Security Apps project work proceeding in accordance with the original Security Apps project schedule?

410. How detailed should a Security Apps project get?

411. Are activities connected because logic dictates the order in which others occur?

412. How do you manage Security Apps project Risk?

413. What is risk?

414. Are all remaining durations correct?

415. Why or why not?

416. If there are any qualifying green components to this Security Apps project, what portion of the total Security Apps project cost is green?

417. What is the most mis-scheduled part of process?

418. Schedule/cost recovery?

419. Are the original Security Apps project schedule and budget realistic?

420. How can slack be negative?

421. How much slack is available in the Security Apps project?

422. Meet requirements?

423. What is the purpose of a Security Apps project schedule?

424. Master Security Apps project schedule?

425. What is risk management?

2.20 Cost Management Plan: Security Apps

426. Eac -estimate at completion, what is the total job expected to cost?

427. Are post milestone Security Apps project reviews (PMPR) conducted with your organization at least once a year?

428. Will the earned value reporting interface between time and cost management?

429. Were stakeholders aware and supportive of the principles and practices of modern software estimation?

430. Similar Security Apps projects?

431. Have activity relationships and interdependencies within tasks been adequately identified?

432. Are cause and effect determined for risks when others occur?

433. The definition of the Security Apps project scope what needs to be accomplished?

434. Are all resource assumptions documented?

435. Does the Security Apps project have a formal Security Apps project Charter?

436. Have all team members been part of identifying risks?

437. Are the results of quality assurance reviews provided to affected groups & individuals?

438. Are change requests logged and managed?

439. Are changes in deliverable commitments agreed to by all affected groups & individuals?

440. Has a capability assessment been conducted?

441. Published materials?

442. What is the work breakdown structure for the Security Apps project?

443. Are estimating assumptions and constraints captured?

2.21 Activity Cost Estimates: Security Apps

444. What makes a good expected result statement?

445. How quickly can the task be done with the skills available?

446. What is included in indirect cost being allocated?

447. How many activities should you have?

448. What cost data should be used to estimate costs during the 2-year follow-up period?

449. Based on your Security Apps project communication management plan, what worked well?

450. What is procurement?

451. Where can you get activity reports?

452. What happens if you cannot produce the documentation for the single audit?

453. What areas does the group agree are the biggest success on the Security Apps project?

454. How and when do you enter into Security Apps project Procurement Management?

455. What procedures are put in place regarding

bidding and cost comparisons, if any?

456. How do you change activities?

457. Did the consultant work with local staff to develop local capacity?

458. Will you use any tools, such as Security Apps project management software, to assist in capturing Earned Value metrics?

459. How do you fund change orders?

460. How do you treat administrative costs in the activity inventory?

461. Measurable - are the targets measurable?

462. What is the activity recast of the budget?

463. When do you enter into PPM?

2.22 Cost Estimating Worksheet: Security Apps

464. What additional Security Apps project(s) could be initiated as a result of this Security Apps project?

465. What is the purpose of estimating?

466. What costs are to be estimated?

467. How will the results be shared and to whom?

468. What can be included?

469. What is the estimated labor cost today based upon this information?

470. Can a trend be established from historical performance data on the selected measure and are the criteria for using trend analysis or forecasting methods met?

471. What happens to any remaining funds not used?

472. Identify the timeframe necessary to monitor progress and collect data to determine how the selected measure has changed?

473. Does the Security Apps project provide innovative ways for stakeholders to overcome obstacles or deliver better outcomes?

474. What will others want?

475. Is the Security Apps project responsive to community need?

476. Who is best positioned to know and assist in identifying corresponding factors?

477. Will the Security Apps project collaborate with the local community and leverage resources?

478. Is it feasible to establish a control group arrangement?

479. Ask: are others positioned to know, are others credible, and will others cooperate?

2.23 Cost Baseline: Security Apps

480. On budget?

481. What is the reality?

482. Have all approved changes to the cost baseline been identified and impact on the Security Apps project documented?

483. For what purpose ?

484. Are there contingencies or conditions related to the acceptance?

485. Are you asking management for something as a result of this update?

486. Impact to environment?

487. Does it impact schedule, cost, quality?

488. What strengths do you have?

489. Verify business objectives. Are others appropriate, and well-articulated?

490. Pcs for your new business. what would the life cycle costs be?

491. Is there anything unique in this Security Apps projects scope statement that will affect resources?

492. What threats might prevent you from getting

there?

493. Vac -variance at completion, how much over/ under budget do you expect to be?

494. Has the appropriate access to relevant data and analysis capability been granted?

495. Should a more thorough impact analysis be conducted?

496. Is the requested change request a result of changes in other Security Apps project(s)?

497. How fast?

498. What deliverables come first?

2.24 Quality Management Plan: Security Apps

499. How do senior leaders review organizational performance?

500. How does your organization address regulatory, legal, and ethical compliance?

501. List your organizations customer contact standards that employees are expected to maintain. How are corresponding standards measured?

502. Who gets results of work?

503. Have adequate resources been provided by management to ensure Security Apps project success?

504. Do trained quality assurance auditors conduct the audits as defined in the Quality Management Plan and scheduled by the Security Apps project manager?

505. What is quality and how will you ensure it?

506. What other teams / processes would be impacted by changes to the current process, and how?

507. How are deviations from procedures handled?

508. Can the requirements be traced to the appropriate components of the solution, as well as test scripts?

509. Is staff trained on the software technologies that are being used on the Security Apps project?

510. How do senior leaders create your organizational focus on customers and other stakeholders?

511. What methods are used?

512. Are you following the quality standards?

513. Results Available?

514. How do senior leaders create and communicate values and performance expectations?

515. If it is out of compliance, should the process be amended or should the Plan be amended?

516. What is the Quality Management Plan?

517. What are you trying to accomplish?

2.25 Quality Metrics: Security Apps

518. Was review conducted per standard protocols?

519. What forces exist that would cause them to change?

520. Is quality culture a competitive advantage?

521. What metrics do you measure?

522. How do you calculate corresponding metrics?

523. What is the benchmark?

524. Can visual measures help you to filter visualizations of interest?

525. Was the overall quality better or worse than previous products?

526. Is there a set of procedures to capture, analyze and act on quality metrics?

527. How exactly do you define when differences exist?

528. There are many reasons to shore up quality-related metrics, and what metrics are important?

529. How effective are your security tests?

530. When will the Final Guidance will be issued?

531. Are applicable standards referenced and available?

532. Subjective quality component: customer satisfaction, how do you measure it?

533. Are there any open risk issues?

534. How does one achieve stability?

535. Is there alignment within your organization on definitions?

2.26 Process Improvement Plan: Security Apps

536. Who should prepare the process improvement action plan?

537. What personnel are the coaches for your initiative?

538. Have the supporting tools been developed or acquired?

539. How do you measure?

540. Management commitment at all levels?

541. Why do you want to achieve the goal?

542. Have storage and access mechanisms and procedures been determined?

543. What actions are needed to address the problems and achieve the goals?

544. What makes people good SPI coaches?

545. Where do you focus?

546. Have the frequency of collection and the points in the process where measurements will be made been determined?

547. Why quality management?

548. What is the test-cycle concept?

549. Are you meeting the quality standards?

550. Where do you want to be?

551. To elicit goal statements, do you ask a question such as, What do you want to achieve?

552. Does your process ensure quality?

553. Everyone agrees on what process improvement is, right?

554. How do you manage quality?

555. What personnel are the change agents for your initiative?

2.27 Responsibility Assignment Matrix: Security Apps

556. All cwbs elements specified for external reporting?

557. Most people let you know when others re too busy, and are others really too busy?

558. Is accountability placed at the lowest-possible level within the Security Apps project so that decisions can be made at that level?

559. What will the work cost?

560. Competencies and craftsmanship – what competencies are necessary and what level?

561. Are the bases and rates for allocating costs from each indirect pool consistently applied?

562. Are people afraid to let you know when others are under allocated?

563. Budgeted cost for work performed?

564. Identify potential or actual budget-based and time-based schedule variances?

565. Are all elements of indirect expense identified to overhead cost budgets of Security Apps projections?

566. The total budget for the contract (including

estimates for authorized and unpriced work)?

567. Undistributed budgets, if any?

568. Are management actions taken to reduce indirect costs when there are significant adverse variances?

569. What do you need to implement earned value management?

570. Are meaningful indicators identified for use in measuring the status of cost and schedule performance?

571. Budgeted cost for work scheduled?

572. How can this help you with team building?

573. Too many is: do all the identified roles need to be routinely informed or only in exceptional circumstances?

2.28 Roles and Responsibilities: Security Apps

574. What should you do now to prepare yourself for a promotion, increased responsibilities or a different job?

575. Does your vision/mission support a culture of quality data?

576. What specific behaviors did you observe?

577. What should you highlight for improvement?

578. Concern: where are you limited or have no authority, where you can not influence?

579. What should you do now to ensure that you are meeting all expectations of your current position?

580. Who: who is involved?

581. Key conclusions and recommendations: Are conclusions and recommendations relevant and acceptable?

582. Is there a training program in place for stakeholders covering expectations, roles and responsibilities and any addition knowledge others need to be good stakeholders?

583. What should you do now to ensure that you are exceeding expectations and excelling in your current

position?

584. Do you take the time to clearly define roles and responsibilities on Security Apps project tasks?

585. Once the responsibilities are defined for the Security Apps project, have the deliverables, roles and responsibilities been clearly communicated to every participant?

586. What is working well?

587. What are your major roles and responsibilities in the area of performance measurement and assessment?

588. Are your budgets supportive of a culture of quality data?

589. What areas of supervision are challenging for you?

590. Who is involved?

591. Required skills, knowledge, experience?

592. Are governance roles and responsibilities documented?

593. Who is responsible for each task?

2.29 Human Resource Management Plan: Security Apps

594. Where is your organization headed?

595. How are you going to ensure that you have a well motivated workforce?

596. Account for the purpose of this Security Apps project by describing, at a high-level, what will be done. What is this Security Apps project aiming to achieve?

597. Is there a Quality Management Plan?

598. Are vendor invoices audited for accuracy before payment?

599. What communication items need improvement?

600. Has a resource management plan been created?

601. Is it standard practice to formally commit stakeholders to the Security Apps project via agreements?

602. What are the Staffing Requirements?

603. How does the proposed individual meet each requirement?

604. What areas does the group agree are the biggest success on the Security Apps project?

605. Are vendor contract reports, reviews and visits conducted periodically?

606. Has your organization readiness assessment been conducted?

607. Are tasks tracked by hours?

608. Are milestone deliverables effectively tracked and compared to Security Apps project plan?

609. Does the Security Apps project have a Statement of Work?

610. Have all unresolved risks been documented?

2.30 Communications Management Plan: Security Apps

611. Do you feel more overwhelmed by stakeholders?

612. Who will use or be affected by the result of a Security Apps project?

613. Do you have members of your team responsible for certain stakeholders?

614. Are you constantly rushing from meeting to meeting?

615. Do you feel a register helps?

616. Are there potential barriers between the team and the stakeholder?

617. Who were proponents/opponents?

618. Is there an important stakeholder who is actively opposed and will not receive messages?

619. Who is the stakeholder?

620. What steps can you take for a positive relationship?

621. Are others needed?

622. What data is going to be required?

623. Who to share with?

624. What is Security Apps project communications management?

625. Do you prepare stakeholder engagement plans?

626. Is the stakeholder role recognized by your organization?

627. What communications method?

628. Who did you turn to if you had questions?

629. Do you ask; can you recommend others for you to talk with about this initiative?

630. Are others part of the communications management plan?

2.31 Risk Management Plan: Security Apps

631. Are the required plans included, such as nonstructural flood risk management plans?

632. Does the customer have a solid idea of what is required?

633. What is the likelihood?

634. How is risk identification performed?

635. Are some people working on multiple Security Apps projects?

636. Are the participants able to keep up with the workload?

637. Risk may be made during which step of risk management?

638. Is this an issue, action item, question or a risk?

639. Who/what can assist?

640. Are you working on the right risks?

641. Do requirements demand the use of new analysis, design, or testing methods?

642. How much risk protection can you afford?

643. Was an original risk assessment/risk management plan completed?

644. How will the Security Apps project know if your organizations risk response actions were effective?

645. How is the audit profession changing?

646. Where are you confronted with risks during the business phases?

647. Risk categories: what are the main categories of risks that should be addressed on this Security Apps project?

648. Is the customer willing to commit significant time to the requirements gathering process?

649. Do you manage the process through use of metrics?

650. Are end-users enthusiastically committed to the Security Apps project and the system/product to be built?

2.32 Risk Register: Security Apps

651. Manageability – have mitigations to the risk been identified?

652. What could prevent you delivering on the strategic program objectives and what is being done to mitigate corresponding issues?

653. Methodology: how will risk management be performed on this Security Apps project?

654. Amongst the action plans and recommendations that you have to introduce are there some that could stop or delay the overall program?

655. Severity Prediction?

656. Are there other alternative controls that could be implemented?

657. Technology risk -is the Security Apps project technically feasible?

658. Who needs to know about this?

659. What should the audit role be in establishing a risk management process?

660. Cost/benefit – how much will the proposed mitigations cost and how does this cost compare with the potential cost of the risk event/situation should it occur?

661. What can be done about it?

662. When will it happen?

663. What is the probability and impact of the risk occurring?

664. Financial risk -can your organization afford to undertake the Security Apps project?

665. What should you do when?

666. What is the reason for current performance gaps and do the risks and opportunities identified previously account for this?

667. What are the major risks facing the Security Apps project?

668. Schedule impact/severity estimated range (workdays) assume the event happens, what is the potential impact?

2.33 Probability and Impact Assessment: Security Apps

669. Management -what contingency plans do you have if the risk becomes a reality?

670. To what extent is the chosen technology maturing?

671. Have top software and customer managers formally committed to support the Security Apps project?

672. Are flexibility and reuse paramount?

673. Do you have specific methods that you use for each phase of the process?

674. Are the risk data timely and relevant?

675. What can you do about it?

676. How much risk do others need to take?

677. Who will be responsible for a slippage?

678. Why has this particular mode of contracting been chosen?

679. How will the consumption pattern change?

680. Assumptions analysis -what assumptions have you made or been given about your Security Apps

project?

681. How will economic events and trends likely affect the Security Apps project?

682. Monitoring of the overall Security Apps project status – are there any changes in the Security Apps project that can effect and cause new possible risks?

683. Have customers been involved fully in the definition of requirements?

684. What are the current requirements of the customer?

685. What things are likely to change?

686. Assuming that you have identified a number of risks in the Security Apps project, how would you prioritize them?

687. What will be the impact or consequence if the risk occurs?

2.34 Probability and Impact Matrix: Security Apps

688. Is Security Apps project scope stable?

689. The customer requests a change to the Security Apps project that would increase the Security Apps project risk. Which should you do before ass the others?

690. What are the levels of understanding of the future users of this technology?

691. Have you worked with the customer in the past?

692. What are the channels available for distribution to the customer?

693. What are data sources?

694. Is a software Security Apps project management tool available?

695. Are there alternative opinions/solutions/ processes you should explore?

696. Can you stabilize dynamic risk factors?

697. What are the chances the risk events will occur?

698. How do you manage Security Apps project Risk?

699. What can you use the analyzed risks for?

700. Do you have a consistent repeatable process that is actually used?

701. Which of the risk factors can be avoided altogether?

702. How are you working with risks?

2.35 Risk Data Sheet: Security Apps

703. What are the main threats to your existence?

704. What will be the consequences if the risk happens?

705. How can hazards be reduced?

706. Do effective diagnostic tests exist?

707. What actions can be taken to eliminate or remove risk?

708. What if client refuses?

709. Has a sensitivity analysis been carried out?

710. What is the environment within which you operate (social trends, economic, community values, broad based participation, national directions etc.)?

711. Risk of what?

712. What do you know?

713. Potential for recurrence?

714. What are you weak at and therefore need to do better?

715. If it happens, what are the consequences?

716. Whom do you serve (customers)?

717. What will be the consequences if it happens?

718. What do people affected think about the need for, and practicality of preventive measures?

719. What are the main opportunities available to you that you should grab while you can?

720. What were the Causes that contributed?

721. Is the data sufficiently specified in terms of the type of failure being analyzed, and its frequency or probability?

722. How reliable is the data source?

2.36 Procurement Management Plan: Security Apps

723. How and when do you enter into Security Apps project Procurement Management?

724. Are Security Apps project team members committed fulltime?

725. How will you coordinate Procurement with aspects of the Security Apps project?

726. Does the resource management plan include a personnel development plan?

727. Does the schedule include Security Apps project management time and change request analysis time?

728. Was your organizations estimating methodology being used and followed?

729. Has Security Apps project success criteria been defined?

730. Is the quality assurance team identified?

731. Is the current scope of the Security Apps project substantially different than that originally defined?

732. Is there a procurement management plan in place?

733. Is there a requirements change management

processes in place?

734. Have the key elements of a coherent Security Apps project management strategy been established?

735. Has a structured approach been used to break work effort into manageable components (WBS)?

736. In which phase of the Acquisition Process Cycle does source qualifications reside?

737. Are key risk mitigation strategies added to the Security Apps project schedule?

738. Does all Security Apps project documentation reside in a common repository for easy access?

2.37 Source Selection Criteria: Security Apps

739. What are the steps in performing a cost/tech tradeoff?

740. What does a sample rating scale look like?

741. Can you identify proposed teaming partners and/ or subcontractors and consider the nature and extent of proposed involvement in satisfying the Security Apps project requirements?

742. How and when do you enter into Security Apps project Procurement Management?

743. When must you conduct a debriefing?

744. What should communications be used to accomplish?

745. Are resultant proposal revisions allowed?

746. What is cost analysis and when should it be performed?

747. Is there collaboration among your evaluators?

748. When and what information can be considered with offerors regarding past performance?

749. What is price analysis and when should it be performed?

750. What should preproposal conferences accomplish?

751. How are clarifications and communications appropriately used?

752. What are the most critical evaluation criteria that prove to be tiebreakers in the evaluation of proposals?

753. Are there any specific considerations that precludes offers from being selected as the awardee?

754. What documentation should be used to support the selection decision?

755. Does the evaluation of any change include an impact analysis; how will the change affect the scope, time, cost, and quality of the goods or services being provided?

756. Are considerations anticipated?

757. What can not be disclosed?

758. How will you evaluate offerors proposals?

2.38 Stakeholder Management Plan: Security Apps

759. Does the Security Apps project have a formal Security Apps project Charter?

760. What potential impact does the Security Apps project have on the stakeholder?

761. Which impacts could serve as impediments?

762. Is a stakeholder management plan in place?

763. Is an industry recognized mechanized support tool(s) being used for Security Apps project scheduling & tracking?

764. Have stakeholder accountabilities & responsibilities been clearly defined?

765. Is there any form of automated support for Issues Management?

766. What potential impact does the stakeholder have on the Security Apps project?

767. Has the Security Apps project manager been identified?

768. Was trending evident between reviews?

769. Are there nonconformance issues?

770. What preventative action can be taken to reduce the likelihood a risk will be realised?

771. What inspection and testing is to be performed?

772. Where will verification occur, and by whom?

773. What action will be taken once reports have been received?

2.39 Change Management Plan: Security Apps

774. When does it make sense to customize?

775. Where will the funds come from?

776. How badly can information be misinterpreted?

777. Do the proposed users have access to the appropriate documentation?

778. Has the target training audience been identified and nominated?

779. What are the current methods of sharing information and do there need to be new ones developed?

780. What method and medium would you use to announce a message?

781. Which relationships will change?

782. How does the principle of senders and receivers make the Security Apps project communications effort more complex?

783. Who might present the most resistance?

784. What time commitment will this involve?

785. Has a training need analysis been carried out?

786. What prerequisite knowledge do corresponding groups need?

787. Who is the target audience of the piece of information?

788. Who will do the training?

789. Is there a software application relevant to this deliverable?

790. What do you expect the target audience to do, say, think or feel as a result of this communication?

791. Impact of systems implementation on organization change?

792. What is the worst thing that can happen if you chose not to communicate this information?

3.0 Executing Process Group: Security Apps

793. How many different communication channels does the Security Apps project team have?

794. How could stakeholders negatively impact your Security Apps project?

795. How is Security Apps project performance information created and distributed?

796. Based on your Security Apps project communication management plan, what worked well?

797. What are the main parts of the scope statement?

798. Is the Security Apps project performing better or worse than planned?

799. What will you do to minimize the impact should a risk event occur?

800. How will you avoid scope creep?

801. What Security Apps projects and services are in the portfolio of your organization?

802. What are deliverables of your Security Apps project?

803. What are the typical Security Apps project

management skills?

804. Is the program supported by national and/or local organizations?

805. Are the necessary foundations in place to ensure the sustainability of the results of the programme?

806. How can your organization use a weighted decision matrix to evaluate proposals as part of source selection?

807. Will new hardware or software be required for servers or client machines?

808. Who will provide training?

809. What areas does the group agree are the biggest success on the Security Apps project?

810. What areas were overlooked on this Security Apps project?

3.1 Team Member Status Report: Security Apps

811. Does your organization have the means (staff, money, contract, etc.) to produce or to acquire the product, good, or service?

812. Are the products of your organizations Security Apps projects meeting customers objectives?

813. Do you have an Enterprise Security Apps project Management Office (EPMO)?

814. How can you make it practical?

815. Does the product, good, or service already exist within your organization?

816. Are your organizations Security Apps projects more successful over time?

817. How will resource planning be done?

818. Are the attitudes of staff regarding Security Apps project work improving?

819. What specific interest groups do you have in place?

820. How does this product, good, or service meet the needs of the Security Apps project and your organization as a whole?

821. When a teams productivity and success depend on collaboration and the efficient flow of information, what generally fails them?

822. Does every department have to have a Security Apps project Manager on staff?

823. Will the staff do training or is that done by a third party?

824. The problem with Reward & Recognition Programs is that the truly deserving people all too often get left out. How can you make it practical?

825. How it is to be done?

826. Is there evidence that staff is taking a more professional approach toward management of your organizations Security Apps projects?

827. How much risk is involved?

828. Why is it to be done?

829. What is to be done?

3.2 Change Request: Security Apps

830. How many lines of code must be changed to implement the change?

831. Who is responsible for the implementation and monitoring of all measures?

832. Who has responsibility for approving and ranking changes?

833. What kind of information about the change request needs to be captured?

834. How do you get changes (code) out in a timely manner?

835. Has the change been highlighted and documented in the CSCI?

836. Is it feasible to use requirements attributes as predictors of reliability?

837. What are the duties of the change control team?

838. What are the Impacts to your organization?

839. Are there requirements attributes that are strongly related to the occurrence of defects and failures?

840. What is the function of the change control committee?

841. Who needs to approve change requests?

842. How does your organization control changes before and after software is released to a customer?

843. How do team members communicate with each other?

844. Change request coordination ?

845. How shall the implementation of changes be recorded?

846. Customer acceptance plan how will the customer verify the change has been implemented successfully?

847. Has a formal technical review been conducted to assess technical correctness?

848. Why do you want to have a change control system?

3.3 Change Log: Security Apps

849. Who initiated the change request?

850. How does this relate to the standards developed for specific business processes?

851. Where do changes come from?

852. How does this change affect the timeline of the schedule?

853. How does this change affect scope?

854. Is the submitted change a new change or a modification of a previously approved change?

855. Is this a mandatory replacement?

856. When was the request submitted?

857. Is the requested change request a result of changes in other Security Apps project(s)?

858. Do the described changes impact on the integrity or security of the system?

859. Is the change request within Security Apps project scope?

860. Does the suggested change request seem to represent a necessary enhancement to the product?

861. Is the change backward compatible without

limitations?

862. When was the request approved?

863. Will the Security Apps project fail if the change request is not executed?

864. Does the suggested change request represent a desired enhancement to the products functionality?

865. Is the change request open, closed or pending?

3.4 Decision Log: Security Apps

866. At what point in time does loss become unacceptable?

867. How consolidated and comprehensive a story can you tell by capturing currently available incident data in a central location and through a log of key decisions during an incident?

868. Behaviors; what are guidelines that the team has identified that will assist them with getting the most out of team meetings?

869. With whom was the decision shared or considered?

870. What are the cost implications?

871. Is everything working as expected?

872. How effective is maintaining the log at facilitating organizational learning?

873. Is your opponent open to a non-traditional workflow, or will it likely challenge anything you do?

874. How do you define success?

875. How does provision of information, both in terms of content and presentation, influence acceptance of alternative strategies?

876. Who is the decisionmaker?

877. Does anything need to be adjusted?

878. What makes you different or better than others companies selling the same thing?

879. How do you know when you are achieving it?

880. Who will be given a copy of this document and where will it be kept?

881. Do strategies and tactics aimed at less than full control reduce the costs of management or simply shift the cost burden?

882. What is the average size of your matters in an applicable measurement?

883. What is the line where eDiscovery ends and document review begins?

884. What was the rationale for the decision?

885. It becomes critical to track and periodically revisit both operational effectiveness; Are you noticing all that you need to, and are you interpreting what you see effectively?

3.5 Quality Audit: Security Apps

886. How does your organization know that the quality of its supervisors is appropriately effective and constructive?

887. How does your organization know that its systems for providing high quality consultancy services to external parties are appropriately effective and constructive?

888. How does your organization know that its staff have appropriate access to a fair and effective grievance process?

889. What is your organizations greatest strength?

890. Does the report read coherently?

891. How does your organization know that its system for managing intellectual property issues is appropriately effective, constructive and fair?

892. How do you indicate the extent to which your personnel would be expected to contribute to the work effort?

893. Does your organization have set of goals, objectives, strategies and targets that are clearly understood by the Board and staff?

894. Are all staff empowered and encouraged to contribute to ongoing improvement efforts?

895. Has a written procedure been established to identify devices during all stages of receipt, reconditioning, distribution and installation so that mix-ups are prevented?

896. How does your organization know that its processes for managing severance are appropriately effective, constructive and fair?

897. What data about organizational performance is routinely collected and reported?

898. Are all complaints involving the possible failure of a device, labeling, or packaging to meet any of its specifications reviewed, evaluated, and investigated?

899. Are salvageable and salvaged medical devices stored in a manner to prevent damage and/or contamination?

900. How does your organization know that its Governance system is appropriately effective and constructive?

901. Is the reports overall tone appropriate?

902. How does your organization know that its staff placements are appropriately effective and constructive in relation to program-related learning outcomes?

903. How does your organization know that its staff are presenting original work, and properly acknowledging the work of others?

904. How is the Strategic Plan (and other plans)

reviewed and revised?

905. How does your organization know that its relationships with the community at large are appropriately effective and constructive?

3.6 Team Directory: Security Apps

906. Process decisions: how well was task order work performed?

907. How will you accomplish and manage the objectives?

908. Process decisions: is work progressing on schedule and per contract requirements?

909. When will you produce deliverables?

910. What needs to be communicated?

911. Process decisions: do job conditions warrant additional actions to collect job information and document on-site activity?

912. How do unidentified risks impact the outcome of the Security Apps project?

913. Process decisions: are there any statutory or regulatory issues relevant to the timely execution of work?

914. Is construction on schedule?

915. Contract requirements complied with?

916. Who are the Team Members?

917. Where will the product be used and/or delivered or built when appropriate?

918. How does the team resolve conflicts and ensure tasks are completed?

919. Have you decided when to celebrate the Security Apps projects completion date?

920. Who will be the stakeholders on your next Security Apps project?

921. How and in what format should information be presented?

922. Do purchase specifications and configurations match requirements?

923. Where should the information be distributed?

924. Who are your stakeholders (customers, sponsors, end users, team members)?

3.7 Team Operating Agreement: Security Apps

925. Did you prepare participants for the next meeting?

926. Is compensation based on team and individual performance?

927. Do you call or email participants to ensure understanding, follow-through and commitment to the meeting outcomes?

928. How does teaming fit in with overall organizational goals and meet organizational needs?

929. Do you upload presentation materials in advance and test the technology?

930. What is your unique contribution to your organization?

931. Conflict resolution: how will disputes and other conflicts be mediated or resolved?

932. Are there influences outside the team that may affect performance, and if so, have you identified and addressed them?

933. Must your team members rely on the expertise of other members to complete tasks?

934. Are there differences in access to communication

and collaboration technology based on team member location?

935. Are there more than two functional areas represented by your team?

936. How will group handle unplanned absences?

937. Do team members need to frequently communicate as a full group to make timely decisions?

938. Have you set the goals and objectives of the team?

939. Do you post any action items, due dates, and responsibilities on the team website?

940. Do you prevent individuals from dominating the meeting?

941. What is the anticipated procedure (recruitment, solicitation of volunteers, or assignment) for selecting team members?

942. How will you resolve conflict efficiently and respectfully?

943. What individual strengths does each team member bring to the group?

3.8 Team Performance Assessment: Security Apps

944. How do you recognize and praise members for contributions?

945. To what degree do all members feel responsible for all agreed-upon measures?

946. To what degree do members articulate the goals beyond the team membership?

947. Lack of method variance in self-reported affect and perceptions at work: Reality or artifact?

948. How hard do you try to make a good selection?

949. To what degree can team members vigorously define the teams purpose in considerations with others who are not part of the functioning team?

950. To what degree does the teams purpose constitute a broader, deeper aspiration than just accomplishing short-term goals?

951. What is method variance?

952. How much interpersonal friction is there in your team?

953. To what degree are staff involved as partners in the improvement process?

954. To what degree are corresponding categories of skills either actually or potentially represented across the membership?

955. To what degree can all members engage in open and interactive considerations?

956. When does the medium matter?

957. To what degree does the teams purpose contain themes that are particularly meaningful and memorable?

958. Effects of crew composition on crew performance: Does the whole equal the sum of its parts?

959. To what degree does the teams approach to its work allow for modification and improvement over time?

960. How does Security Apps project termination impact Security Apps project team members?

961. To what degree can team members meet frequently enough to accomplish the teams ends?

962. To what degree are sub-teams possible or necessary?

963. What structural changes have you made or are you preparing to make?

3.9 Team Member Performance Assessment: Security Apps

964. What future plans (e.g., modifications) do you have for your program?

965. To what degree do team members frequently explore the teams purpose and its implications?

966. How is your organizations Strategic Management System tied to performance measurement?

967. What are top priorities?

968. In what areas would you like to concentrate your knowledge and resources?

969. To what degree does the team possess adequate membership to achieve its ends?

970. How do you implement Cost Reduction?

971. To what degree are the goals ambitious?

972. Does adaptive training work?

973. How will you identify your Team Leaders?

974. How are performance measures and associated incentives developed?

975. To what degree is the team cognizant of small wins to be celebrated along the way?

976. Are there any safeguards to prevent intentional or unintentional rating errors?

977. Who receives a benchmark visit?

978. How often should assessments be conducted?

979. To what degree are the relative importance and priority of the goals clear to all team members?

980. How do you determine which data are the most important to use, analyze, or review?

981. Are the goals SMART ?

982. What variables that affect team members achievement are within your control?

3.10 Issue Log: Security Apps

983. How much time does it take to do it?

984. Which team member will work with each stakeholder?

985. How often do you engage with stakeholders?

986. Who do you turn to if you have questions?

987. Who needs to know and how much?

988. What date was the issue resolved?

989. How is this initiative related to other portfolios, programs, or Security Apps projects?

990. Are the stakeholders getting the information they need, are they consulted, are concerns addressed?

991. What is the impact on the risks?

992. Who have you worked with in past, similar initiatives?

993. What would have to change?

994. What does the stakeholder need from the team?

995. Which stakeholders can influence others?

996. Where do team members get information?

997. What effort will a change need?

998. Who reported the issue?

999. What steps can you take for positive relationships?

1000. Who is the issue assigned to?

4.0 Monitoring and Controlling Process Group: Security Apps

1001. How is Agile Security Apps project Management done?

1002. Purpose: toward what end is the evaluation being conducted?

1003. What do they need to know about the Security Apps project?

1004. What kinds of things in particular are you looking for data on?

1005. Is progress on outcomes due to your program?

1006. Mitigate. what will you do to minimize the impact should a risk event occur?

1007. Feasibility: how much money, time, and effort can you put into this?

1008. Do clients benefit (change) from the services?

1009. Use: how will they use the information?

1010. Change, where should you look for problems?

1011. How were collaborations developed, and how are they sustained?

1012. Are the services being delivered?

1013. Key stakeholders to work with. How many potential communications channels exist on the Security Apps project?

1014. How do you monitor progress?

1015. Were sponsors and decision makers available when needed outside regularly scheduled meetings?

1016. Propriety: who needs to be involved in the evaluation to be ethical?

1017. User: who wants the information and what are they interested in?

4.1 Project Performance Report: Security Apps

1018. To what degree is the information network consistent with the structure of the formal organization?

1019. To what degree can the team ensure that all members are individually and jointly accountable for the teams purpose, goals, approach, and work-products?

1020. To what degree do individual skills and abilities match task demands?

1021. How will procurement be coordinated with other Security Apps project aspects, such as scheduling and performance reporting?

1022. To what degree will each member have the opportunity to advance his or her professional skills in all three of the above categories while contributing to the accomplishment of the teams purpose and goals?

1023. To what degree will the team ensure that all members equitably share the work essential to the success of the team?

1024. To what degree are the demands of the task compatible with and converge with the relationships of the informal organization?

1025. To what degree does the teams work approach

provide opportunity for members to engage in results-based evaluation?

1026. To what degree are the skill areas critical to team performance present?

1027. To what degree does the formal organization make use of individual resources and meet individual needs?

1028. What is in it for you?

1029. To what degree are the goals realistic?

1030. To what degree can the cognitive capacity of individuals accommodate the flow of information?

1031. How can Security Apps project sustainability be maintained?

1032. To what degree are the structures of the formal organization consistent with the behaviors in the informal organization?

4.2 Variance Analysis: Security Apps

1033. Are procedures for variance analysis documented and consistently applied at the control account level and selected WBS and organizational levels at least monthly as a routine task?

1034. How does your organization allocate the cost of shared expenses and services?

1035. Is work properly classified as measured effort, LOE, or apportioned effort and appropriately separated?

1036. Who are responsible for overhead performance control of related costs?

1037. What is your organizations rationale for sharing expenses and services between business segments?

1038. Are significant decision points, constraints, and interfaces identified as key milestones?

1039. Is data disseminated to the contractors management timely, accurate, and usable?

1040. What business event caused the fluctuation?

1041. How are material, labor, and overhead standards set?

1042. Are the overhead pools formally and adequately identified?

1043. Are there changes in the overhead pool and/or organization structures?

1044. How do you evaluate the impact of schedule changes, work around, et?

1045. Are indirect costs charged to the appropriate indirect pools and incurring organization?

1046. What is the budgeted cost for work scheduled?

1047. At what point should variances be isolated and brought to the attention of the management?

1048. Are all elements of indirect expense identified to overhead cost budgets of Security Apps projections?

1049. Is the market likely to continue to grow at this rate next year?

1050. Are control accounts opened and closed based on the start and completion of work contained therein?

4.3 Earned Value Status: Security Apps

1051. How does this compare with other Security Apps projects?

1052. Where is evidence-based earned value in your organization reported?

1053. Where are your problem areas?

1054. When is it going to finish?

1055. What is the unit of forecast value?

1056. Verification is a process of ensuring that the developed system satisfies the stakeholders agreements and specifications; Are you building the product right? What do you verify?

1057. Are you hitting your Security Apps projects targets?

1058. If earned value management (EVM) is so good in determining the true status of a Security Apps project and Security Apps project its completion, why is it that hardly any one uses it in information systems related Security Apps projects?

1059. Validation is a process of ensuring that the developed system will actually achieve the stakeholders desired outcomes; Are you building the right product? What do you validate?

1060. How much is it going to cost by the finish?

1061. Earned value can be used in almost any Security Apps project situation and in almost any Security Apps project environment. it may be used on large Security Apps projects, medium sized Security Apps projects, tiny Security Apps projects (in cut-down form), complex and simple Security Apps projects and in any market sector. some people, of course, know all about earned value, they have used it for years - but perhaps not as effectively as they could have?

4.4 Risk Audit: Security Apps

1062. Do you have a procedure for dealing with complaints?

1063. Number of users of the product?

1064. Is the customer technically sophisticated in the product area?

1065. For paid staff, does your organization comply with the minimum conditions for employment and/or the applicable modern award?

1066. Has an event time line been developed?

1067. Are there any forms the staff is required to sign?

1068. Should additional substantive testing be conducted because of the risk audit results?

1069. Have all possible risks/hazards been identified (including injury to staff, damage to equipment, impact on others in the community)?

1070. Are all financial transactions accurately recorded (receipted, banked)?

1071. Assessing risk with analytical procedures: do systemsthinking tools help auditors focus on diagnostic patterns?

1072. Are regular safety inspections made of buildings, grounds and equipment?

1073. Do staff understand the extent of duty of care?

1074. Do you have an understanding of insurance claims processes?

1075. Who audits the auditor?

1076. Are the best people available?

1077. What compliance systems do you have in place to address quality, errors, and outcomes?

1078. To what extent are auditors effective at linking business risks and management assertions?

1079. Do you meet the legislative requirements (for example PAYG, super contributions) for paid employees?

1080. Has risk management been considered when planning an event?

4.5 Contractor Status Report: Security Apps

1081. Are there contractual transfer concerns?

1082. If applicable; describe your standard schedule for new software version releases. Are new software version releases included in the standard maintenance plan?

1083. How long have you been using the services?

1084. What was the final actual cost?

1085. What process manages the contracts?

1086. What was the budget or estimated cost for your organizations services?

1087. What are the minimum and optimal bandwidth requirements for the proposed solution?

1088. Who can list a Security Apps project as organization experience, your organization or a previous employee of your organization?

1089. What was the overall budget or estimated cost?

1090. How is risk transferred?

1091. What is the average response time for answering a support call?

1092. What was the actual budget or estimated cost for your organizations services?

1093. Describe how often regular updates are made to the proposed solution. Are corresponding regular updates included in the standard maintenance plan?

4.6 Formal Acceptance: Security Apps

1094. Do you buy-in installation services?

1095. General estimate of the costs and times to complete the Security Apps project?

1096. Was the Security Apps project work done on time, within budget, and according to specification?

1097. Who would use it?

1098. Was the Security Apps project goal achieved?

1099. What features, practices, and processes proved to be strengths or weaknesses?

1100. Was the Security Apps project managed well?

1101. Did the Security Apps project manager and team act in a professional and ethical manner?

1102. Does it do what Security Apps project team said it would?

1103. Have all comments been addressed?

1104. Was the client satisfied with the Security Apps project results?

1105. How does your team plan to obtain formal acceptance on your Security Apps project?

1106. Do you buy pre-configured systems or build

your own configuration?

1107. What can you do better next time?

1108. What was done right?

1109. What function(s) does it fill or meet?

1110. Did the Security Apps project achieve its MOV?

1111. Do you perform formal acceptance or burn-in tests?

1112. What is the Acceptance Management Process?

1113. What lessons were learned about your Security Apps project management methodology?

5.0 Closing Process Group: Security Apps

1114. What can you do better next time, and what specific actions can you take to improve?

1115. If a risk event occurs, what will you do?

1116. What is the amount of funding and what Security Apps project phases are funded?

1117. What areas does the group agree are the biggest success on the Security Apps project?

1118. Contingency planning. if a risk event occurs, what will you do?

1119. Are there funding or time constraints?

1120. Did the delivered product meet the specified requirements and goals of the Security Apps project?

1121. What is the risk of failure to your organization?

1122. How will staff learn how to use the deliverables?

1123. What level of risk does the proposed budget represent to the Security Apps project?

1124. What areas were overlooked on this Security Apps project?

1125. Did you do things well?

1126. Will the Security Apps project deliverable(s) replace a current asset or group of assets?

1127. Is this a follow-on to a previous Security Apps project?

1128. When will the Security Apps project be done?

1129. Were the outcomes different from the already stated planned?

1130. Just how important is your work to the overall success of the Security Apps project?

5.1 Procurement Audit: Security Apps

1131. Was all the key documentation given to the contracting authority?

1132. Was confidentiality ensured when necessary?

1133. How do you monitor behaviour of procurement staff?

1134. Did the chosen procedure ensure fair competition and transparency?

1135. Is each copy of the purchase order necessary?

1136. Did you consider and evaluate alternatives, like bundling needs with other departments or grouping supplies in separate lots with different characteristics?

1137. Were results of the award procedures published?

1138. Is a cash flow chart prepared and used in determining the timing and term of investments?

1139. Is an appropriated degree of standardization of goods and services respected?

1140. Has your organization fulfilled its obligations related to the payment of social security contributions and taxes?

1141. Are the purchase order forms designed for efficient and simple completion?

1142. Are all initial purchase contracts made by the purchasing organization?

1143. Are there inferior competencies among procurement staff?

1144. Was the suitability of candidates accurately assessed?

1145. Was the performance description adequate to needs and legal requirements?

1146. When you set social or environmental conditions for the performance of the contract, were corresponding compatible with the law and was adequate information given to the candidates?

1147. Are obtained prices/qualities competitive to prices/qualities obtained by other procurement functions/units, comparing obtained or improved value for money?

1148. Do the employees have the necessary skills and experience to carry out procurements efficiently?

1149. Are the responsibilities of the purchasing department clearly defined?

1150. How are you making the audit trail easy to follow?

5.2 Contract Close-Out: Security Apps

1151. Why Outsource?

1152. How does it work?

1153. Are the signers the authorized officials?

1154. Was the contract type appropriate?

1155. What happens to the recipient of services?

1156. How is the contracting office notified of the automatic contract close-out?

1157. Have all acceptance criteria been met prior to final payment to contractors?

1158. Has each contract been audited to verify acceptance and delivery?

1159. Parties: Authorized?

1160. Have all contract records been included in the Security Apps project archives?

1161. What is capture management?

1162. Change in circumstances?

1163. Have all contracts been closed?

1164. Was the contract complete without requiring numerous changes and revisions?

1165. Change in knowledge?

1166. Have all contracts been completed?

1167. Change in attitude or behavior?

1168. How/when used ?

1169. Parties: who is involved?

1170. Was the contract sufficiently clear so as not to result in numerous disputes and misunderstandings?

5.3 Project or Phase Close-Out: Security Apps

1171. Complete yes or no?

1172. What are the mandatory communication needs for each stakeholder?

1173. When and how were information needs best met?

1174. What could have been improved?

1175. What is this stakeholder expecting?

1176. What was expected from each stakeholder?

1177. Did the delivered product meet the specified requirements and goals of the Security Apps project?

1178. Planned completion date?

1179. What is a Risk?

1180. What was the preferred delivery mechanism?

1181. Was the user/client satisfied with the end product?

1182. What could be done to improve the process?

1183. Was the schedule met?

1184. Who exerted influence that has positively affected or negatively impacted the Security Apps project?

1185. What process was planned for managing issues/risks?

1186. Is there a clear cause and effect between the activity and the lesson learned?

1187. Were risks identified and mitigated?

1188. What benefits or impacts does the stakeholder group expect to obtain as a result of the Security Apps project?

1189. If you were the Security Apps project sponsor, how would you determine which Security Apps project team(s) and/or individuals deserve recognition?

5.4 Lessons Learned: Security Apps

1190. Was sufficient advance training conducted and/or information provided to enable the already stated affected by the changes to adjust to and accommodate them?

1191. What surprises did the team have to deal with?

1192. What is your organizational ideology?

1193. Were any strategies or activities unsuccessful?

1194. How complete and timely were the materials you were provided to decide whether to proceed from one Security Apps project lifecycle phase to the next?

1195. What would you change?

1196. How efficient were Security Apps project team meetings conducted?

1197. What is your organizations performance history?

1198. How well prepared were you to receive Security Apps project deliverables?

1199. What is below the surface?

1200. How will you allocate your funding resources?

1201. What is the impact of tax policy on the case?

1202. Overall, how effective were the efforts to prepare you and your organization for the impact of the product/service of the Security Apps project?

1203. What are the external dependencies?

1204. How did the estimated Security Apps project Budget compare with the total actual expenditures?

1205. How effectively were issues managed on the Security Apps project?

1206. What are the expectations of the individuals?

1207. How often do communications get lost?

Index

CPSIA information can be obtained
at www.ICGtesting.com
Printed in the USA
BVHW071117180719
553828BV00015B/1693/P